Creating Academic Momentum

MONICA:

 THANK YOU FOR ALL THAT
YOU DO IN SUPPORT OF
PERSONALIZED EDUCATION,
& FOR THIS PROJECT TOO!
I'M AFRAID THIS LONG STRUGGLE
WILL REQUIRE YOUR EFFORTS
FOR SOME TIME TO COME.
TAKE CARE.

7/5/2016

Creating Academic Momentum

Realizing the Promise of Performance-Based Education

Michael K. Raible

ROWMAN & LITTLEFIELD
Lanham • Boulder • New York • London

Published by Rowman & Littlefield
A wholly owned subsidary of The Rowman & Littlefield Publishing Group, Inc.
4501 Forbes Boulevard, Suite 200, Lanham, Maryland 20706
www.rowman.com

Unit A, Whitacre Mews, 26-34 Stannary Street, London SE11 4AB

British Library Cataloguing in Publication Information Available

Library of Congress Cataloging-in-Publication Data

Names: Raible, Michael K.
Title: Creating academic momentum : realizing the promise of performance-based education /
    Michael K. Raible.
Description: Lanham, Maryland : Rowman & Littlefield, 2016.
Identifiers: LCCN 2016004769 (print) | LCCN 2016007398 (ebook) | ISBN 9781475821192 (cloth :
    alk. paper) | ISBN 9781475821208 (pbk. : alk. paper) | ISBN 9781475821215 (Electronic)
Subjects: LCSH: Competency-based education—United States.
Classification: LCC LC1032 .R35 2016 (print) | LCC LC1032 (ebook) | DDC 370.11--dc23 | LC
    record available at http://lccn.loc.gov/2016004769

Printed in the United States of America

Contents

Foreword

The idea that there are "no bad questions" is an idea that I would really challenge. Think about the types of questions you ask. Any question that you ask to gain knowledge is a good one, but not all questions are necessarily shaped this way. For example, asking, "Why do we have to do this?" in a tone that is almost dismissive is not a question that is meant to move some forward, but for them to actually stand still.

It is not that we shouldn't ask *why*. But in education, do we ask *why* in pursuit of figuring out ways to become better for our students, or in an effort to *not* move forward? Questions that are to create something better for our students are really the great questions that we should be asking and focusing on as we move forward. Through that process, we as educators model the lifelong learning we so want to see in our students. Learning is not only about gaining knowledge, but about developing one's self.

Yet the worst thing we can do is not ask questions at all. So many administrators walk into new communities, and they either a) try to maintain what already exists, or b) try to change everything immediately with no rhyme or reason. Neither one is a strong strategy. One of the things that I challenge leaders to do is always look with "fresh eyes." What I mean by that is that whether you have been in the building for one month, or ten years, look around and constantly ask "why?"

Sometimes we get so used to the way things have always been done that we do not even think about what possibly could be. What is really interesting about this line of thinking is that it is in all of us. As kids, we are innately curious and look at things with awe and wonder and think of possibilities, as opposed to obstacles. Yet many adults lose this along the way, and in reality, sometimes it's because of a school system that rewards compliance over a child's creativity.

Doing what you are told should not be the standard of excellence in our schools today; questioning, seeing, and creating new possibilities should. Kids can teach adults so much, but there is nothing more powerful than thinking like a child and seeing possibility in front of them. This viewpoint is something we need to embrace.

Innovation in education is more about a mindset than a skill set. This was one of the first things I was reminded of when reading this book and the focus on ways that we "can," instead of ways that we "can't." As you read this book, I encourage you to ask questions, a lot of them, but with the intention of making a new vision the reality. The examples provided throughout this book cannot simply be carbon copied for every school around the world because each community has unique characteristics and needs, yet with that said, there is something in each chapter that will challenge your thinking and help you and your organization to move forward. An innovator doesn't say, "We can't." A true innovator asks, "How can we?" They are about creating solutions, as opposed to simply seeing problems. What opportunities will you create as you move forward?

As Mike says in the book: "Education should provide opportunities, not barriers." For this to happen, we will need to challenge our thinking and continuously ask: "How can we?" Leaders, from any position, find a way forward; that's why they are leaders. See the possibilities and find that way.

George Couros, author of The Innovator's Mindset
Division Principal of Innovative Teaching and Learning
Parkland School Division
Stony Plain, Alberta, Canada

Preface

Heading east after the stoplight on US 68 into Campbellsville, you get the idea that the town is much like many of the other twenty-four towns of about eleven thousand residents in Kentucky. Located in Taylor County, the geographical center of the state, equidistant from Lexington, Louisville, and Bowling Green, it was founded in 1814 and is the county seat. The county has a population of twenty-five thousand.

Over the years, both the town and the county have grown slowly, but steadily. The unemployment rate is 5.3 percent, and the area has its share of corporate taxpayers, including Fruit of the Loom, Amazon, and various furniture makers. There is a huge 8,200-acre lake in the county used for recreational fishing and boating. The county school district serves 2,800 preschool through twelfth grade (P–12) students in a series of older buildings on two campuses (an elementary and a middle/high).

This is not exactly where you would expect to find a public school system that has turned public education into an exercise in disruptive innovation. This small, economically diverse school system is the site of remarkable changes in the educational platform. Taylor County Schools' (TCS) superintendent, Roger Cook, has received regional and national awards for the district's unique interpretation of "performance-based education." By applying this methodology, Taylor County has not had a single student drop out of school for the past six years and counting, a record unsurpassed by the other fourteen thousand school districts in the United States.

Performance-based education refers to the means and methods of instruction, assessment, and placement that are based upon students demonstrating their proficiency with the academic content. If an eight-year-old can demonstrate his or her mastery of the prerequisites for algebra, they are placed in the algebra class. In other contexts, it may be described as *competency-*

based, mastery-based, outcome-based, or *standards-based* education, instruction, and/or learning:

> "The general goal of proficiency-based learning is to ensure that students are acquiring the knowledge and skills that are deemed to be essential to success in school, higher education, careers, and adult life. If students fail to meet expected learning standards, they typically receive additional instruction, practice time, and academic support to help them achieve proficiency or meet the expected standards."[1]

In TCS, instructional delivery is personalized and based upon a student's ability. Grade-level content is seen as the threshold (i.e., the minimum), and there is no ceiling. No child is allowed to fail, and no child is allowed to drop out. TCS, with 60 percent economically disadvantaged students, has outcomes in the 89th percentile in the state, with 60 percent of its high school students testing in the two highest categories (proficient and distinguished) in the state-tested subjects.

The board of education hired Cook in 2009 to replace a retiring superintendent with many years of service. "We didn't realize what we were getting. Over the last three or four years we've become the school system we always hoped we could be," said the board chair in 2015.

From the very beginning, Roger Cook reinvented the status quo. He immediately asked the board to pass a zero-dropouts policy, began acquiring massive amounts of technology, created new programs and new ways of delivering those programs, and challenged every staff member to innovate and become more responsive to the needs of the students. "Forget about thinking outside the box . . . there is no box," he frequently says.

His success is not just due to his own ideas. He relies upon thoughtful collaboration with district leadership staff, school administrators, teachers, students, parents, and community members before attempting to implement innovative programs, carefully tweaking the initiatives at each suggestion. Indeed, when he was asked about which programs hadn't been successful, Cook was stumped. Although he could think of numerous examples of ideas that were "works in progress," he was unable to think of any that had simply failed.

Academic momentum is created for TCS students through a variety of methods:

- No child is held back within an accelerated education program that places students at their level of ability, not by chronological age.
- An early college program allows many high school graduates to enter college as midyear sophomores, saving the class of 2015 an estimated $268,000 in tuition.

- A 1:1 technology initiative gives every student access to at least one handheld electronic device during the school day.
- The district listens and responds to the needs of its students and provides six different ways to learn a wide variety of course content.
- An annual pep rally celebrates academic gains prior to state testing, giving away over $10,000 in prizes to students and also a car to a deserving high school graduate.
- A recognition program continuously validates and recognizes the district's education professionals. This includes cash awards and technical program support for the delivery of academic content on a twenty-first-century platform as well as numerous programs that encourage students to experience the personal satisfaction of being an educator.
- Over sixty hours of targeted and collaborative professional development are provided during the school year, including a protected early release on Friday of almost every week.
- A cyber snow-day program provides course content to students on days when the weather does not permit school attendance, precluding the need for makeup days.
- An array of student enterprises includes an auto detailing service, an online bidding and sales service, an on-campus grocery store, and an Apple-certified break/fix operation for electronic devices at the middle/high school.
- An e-library permits 24/7 access to an extensive collection of written material.
- A diverse career-pathways program includes training in everything from making crème brûlée to getting a pilot's license.
- On-the-job training in local businesses gives students hands-on skill-building experience and an opportunity to acquire the soft skills critical to career success.
- "Just-in-time" remediation serves as a model for the other districts in the state.

Cook credits common sense and hard work for his success and is certain his success can be duplicated in any other district in the country. I believe this as well, and I will use their proven methodologies as the basis for my recommendations. I intend to describe the conditions that will enhance your chances of success if you decide that performance-based education will benefit your students.

The visitor tours of the schools and the district that he leads are scheduled every third Tuesday of the month during the school year and are fast paced and rapid-fire. Cook tends not to linger too long in one area or another. There is only one thing that he cannot tolerate and that is negativity, what he has called "the can'ts," a visitor saying they can't do something new because of budget constraints or internal politics or lack of community or administration support. "They are dead wrong if they think that we didn't have to deal with those issues here," he says.

Cook also travels the country trying to make a difference in education. The presentations that he has made to the National School Boards Association (NSBA) and various other groups from California (Stanford University), Texas (SXSWedu) and Washington, DC (Education Reimagined) are one part information and two parts proselytizing. While he wants people to understand what his district has done, he also wants others to try it because TCS has demonstrated that it works. Unlike many convocation presenters, he is not a theorist; he is a successful practitioner.

However, a district's size, the resources available, the board's appetite for change, the length of tenure of the superintendent, and the community's support are all factors that influence the implementation of something as revolutionary as performance-based education. Every board of education wants their students to be given the best education; every teacher wants their students to do well; and every parent wants their child to be successful. These are the aspirations to which every district leader and every proposal for change must respond.

A mix of visionary and creative leadership, an optimistic and committed educational staff, an engaged group of students, and strong local community support are all necessary ingredients for a successful transition to performance-based learning. This book will discuss those elements, and more, in detail.

Although this is a book about improving the quality of K–12 education, it is not a harangue about our awful current system. The fact is, our system of education is pretty good. The teachers work hard, the administrators are committed, and many of our students do quite well. But we have seemingly reached a plateau in academic outcomes, and recent incremental gains in academic outcomes have been smaller than we would like.

Traditional methodology has not adapted well to the paradigm shift in access to information as a result of technology. Performance-based education seems to be better suited to this change. Coupled with the other changes that Roger Cook and Taylor County have made, it is the logical next step in the evolution of education practice.

This is not a set of step-by-step instructions for the transition to performance-based teaching and learning. It is instead a collection of observations, ideas, and advice about an improved system of program delivery. Where district size, local politics, community involvement, timing, and strategy are factors, they will be mentioned. This is about providing students with the knowledge and skills for a better future. Your own interpretation of performance-based learning might not be exactly that of TCS, but the issues will be much the same.

This is actually the continuation of a discussion that Dr. William Spady and his colleagues began in the 1990s. TCS and Roger Cook have shown that you can successfully interpret the tenets of performance-based education without the complete dismissal of the common assessments administered by the state or the elimination of the grade structure. They have demonstrated that performance-based learning can work within those constraints.

Since this is essentially a problem-solving exercise, let's begin with the phrase that many design thinkers use. "How might we . . . "

- Provide academic leadership that gives our students the tools for success in the twenty-first century?
- Create an organizational structure that supports innovative teaching?
- Deliver content creatively?
- Allow students to progress at their own pace?
- Collaborate to create the best learning for our students?
- Continuously validate our professional educators and our students?
- Use continuous assessments as a learning device?
- Build meaningful professional development into our schedule?
- Develop unique staff positions that actively support our educational delivery?
- Time our remediation to respond to the needs of our students?
- Afford to change our program delivery to a performance-based system?
- Use technology effectively?
- Provide every student with the chance to get college experience?
- Give every student the opportunity to try a career of their choice?
- Recognize and develop high potentials?
- Attract students to the teaching profession?
- Inspire staff and students to do their best work?
- Support the difficult work of our staff and students?
- Create a cooperative culture of academic excellence?
- Transition to our version of performance-based learning?

NOTE

1. Abbott, S. (editor). "Proficiency-Based Learning." The Glossary of Education. August 26, 2014. http://edglossary.org/proficiency-based-learning/ (accessed October 3, 2015).

Part I

Basics

What Makes a Change of This Magnitude Feasible?

Chapter One

Inspiration

Inspiring employees to optimally perform requires a leader who can see be-yond the obvious in people. Inspiration comes not from something that you turn on and off, but rather from constant behavior—triggered through multiple ways—that makes your employees feel that they matter and that you genuinely care.

—Glenn Llopis[1]

Although the board typically creates the vision and mission statements, the district's inspiration originates with the superintendent. Think of the board's vision and mission as setting the guardrails on the road. It is the superintendent who decides what vehicle will be used, how fast it will travel, and what roads will be taken on the journey.

This is not to say that the inspiration is sole-sourced. It must be a synthesis of the needs and values of the community and the district. But once formed, it must be transmitted by the leadership. First and foremost, it must be communicated by the district superintendent and then carried with consistency throughout the system by the executive staff.

For the transition to a version of performance-based learning, the organization's leadership should believe in the power of this platform to deliver successful students. There can be nothing halfhearted about this belief. Both newcomers and veterans should be convinced of the efficacy of the system. When asked what would happen if the superintendent moved on, each and every staff member should say that they would continue to practice performance-based education.

Intent

Inspiration gives everyone in the district a series of simple statements with which to gauge their contribution. The inspiration should be framed in just a few simple statements, such as "no child fails, no child drops out, no child is held back because of their chronological age." Everything that is done or proposed is then measured against those statements.

The Phoenix (Arizona) Elementary School District #1 states in their strategic plan that there are five things that promote student learning: maximizing human capital, enhancing the culture, maximizing financial capacity, state-of-the-art facilities, and responding to the needs of their community. These are a little more difficult to measure precisely, but they still provide strong direction for the district.

Failure

There is a significant amount of baggage attached to failure, particularly in education. It all starts with the letter grades. An "F" on a school performance rating might as well be Hester Prynne's scarlet letter. It is forever emblazoned on our "permanent record."

We think of Thomas A. Edison as a wildly successful and prolific innovator, perhaps one of the smartest inventors of the late nineteenth and early twentieth centuries, even though it is reported that Edison's teachers thought him "too stupid to learn anything."[2]

Even the wizard of Menlo Park, the inventor of the phonograph, the movie projector, and the light bulb, found it difficult to admit to his many failures. "I have not failed 10,000 times—I have successfully found 10,000 ways that will not work." Some of his inventions that did work were not widely accepted. His vote recorder, electric pen, tinfoil phonograph, talking dolls, ore mills and separators, home service clubs, and kinetoscopes were all market failures.[3]

Today's literature about innovation is filled with stories of failures. Most say that if you want to innovate (and you do if you are converting to performance-based learning), then you will need to become more comfortable with the concept. It is after all the way most of us learn.

Process

George Couros is concerned that when we speak of failure in education, we are focusing on the wrong aspect of it. Instead of looking at the outcome, Couros says, the important thing about the failure narrative is the resilience and grit it took to get there, not the success or temporary failure that is the outcome:

Resiliency, in this case, being the ability to come back after a defeat or unsuccessful attempt, and grit, meaning a 'resolve or strength of character.' These are characteristics that are important in the innovative process as we need to continuously develop new and better ways to serve our students.[4]

This makes sense since it is the process and not the outcome that is reproducible and generates the learning. Once you find the "right" outcome, it is no longer necessary to find it again. You move on. But you must use the same grit and resiliency to solve the next problem. Focusing on the result, whether positive or negative, is less important to the learning process than the ability to bounce back after a temporary failure and the grit it takes to try again.

Organizational inspiration is a continuous process as well. As you construct your version of performance-based education, there will be setbacks and temporary diversions. None of these are permanent results. In this case, it really is important to focus on the trends and not the endpoint.

The administration should not claim a monopoly on good ideas and should often encourage the staff to find better ways of doing what needs to be done. Institutional memory is not a substitute for constructive problem solving. If a teacher has a better idea, they must take ownership of the implementation of that idea. There should be no bystanders in your organization, so the enthusiasm for new ideas and the organizational vitality are contagious.

Momentum

No Child Held Back is a book and a course developed by Yovell Badash.[5] The call for academic mastery can be the impetus for providing increasingly challenging academic material and is the basis of accelerated learning. There is no reason to hold a child back strictly on the basis of their chronological age. Platooning and grade-level organization were instituted for efficiency, not because they were effective teaching and learning mechanisms.

Continuous assessment data and analysis will give teachers the tools to evaluate academic progress. As students demonstrate their mastery, they can be accelerated into a more challenging program. This creates academic momentum, and a student who acquires that momentum must not be allowed to stall. A continuation of coursework must be made available to them.

Most of the fuel expended on a journey to the moon is used to escape the inertia of earth's gravity. Once the momentum is achieved, little additional fuel is required to get to the destination. This is true of students as well. The majority of the effort is necessary to create the initial momentum. Once the learning has begun and the student gains learning confidence, it takes less effort to keep them on the learning curve.

Giving Up

There are a variety of reasons why your students choose to give up and leave school. Just as your district should be incredibly stalwart in terms of your vision, you must also be remarkably flexible regarding your methodologies.

Dropping out is the symptom and not the disease. By being nimble and flexible with your programming, you can get those students to decide to stay or return. The issue might be economic (need to earn money), it might be familial (baby on the way), it might be emotional (old and far from earning enough credits).

Failing students are not the only ones who leave. As attention spans have decreased and just being "bored" has become a legitimate excuse for doing something else, some students simply leave school because there is nothing that holds their interest. In many cases, it is the appearance of an inflexible system of program delivery that causes students to draw this conclusion. Respond to all of these issues by solving the problems that they believe prevent them from succeeding—a different schedule, acceleration, access to virtual programming, connecting content to a future career.

Leaders

Most visionary leadership evolves from listening well. But unlike much of the other work described in this book, inspiration has to come from leadership. The vision may be collaborative, but the district superintendent must set the course. This should not be hellfire and brimstone delivered from the bully pulpit.

Jerald Jellison, in *Managing the Dynamics of Change*, describes the "It's a Small World" ride at the Disney theme parks as an example of a group of "diverse (often recalcitrant) individuals" that are turned into a "unified group that is literally singing the same song."

On the ride, individuals of all ages are loaded into boats that move slowly through an environment created and controlled by the Disney designers. You pass displays of children waving and smiling, from all different cultures and all over the world, as the song plays over and over again. The melody and the voices are very positive and the enthusiasm builds as you progress. "The ride's designers not only know how to produce mass change, but they do it by the boatload every few minutes and then repeat it over and over again."

The elements of a change process that Jellison takes from this are repetition, content, style, enthusiasm, and the absence of outside distractions. "So what we have is a simple positive message that is repeated over and over again and an environment that surrounds people with the message while multiplying the emotions of others to heighten the experience."[6]

The superintendent must be able to garner the support of the board, the community, and the staff. This kind of transformational leadership is based upon trust and authenticity. If the performance-based education champion is seen as one who is less than trustworthy or not authentic, it will be difficult to transform the district, even though the value of a program that keeps every student in school is clearly obvious.

Communication

As much as hope has become a modern cliché, it is still the foundation of inspiration. Shane Lopez identifies its three elements: goals, agency, and pathways. Goals give us a destination. Agency gives us the power to change. Pathways give us the routes to our destination.[7]

Goals are not daydreams. Goals are realistic views of what can be accomplished. Wandering without a destination is sometimes exhilarating, but for leaders it cannot be a way of life. The inspiration of a journey cannot be proposed without a destination.

Agency is owning the ability to make changes. If the vision gives us the goal, then it is our own agency that gives us the power to get there. The message here is that everyone is empowered to make this change. Without agency, the work will not get done.

Pathways are the tactics we will employ to accomplish the transition to a performance-based education system. We know there will be obstacles, so we plan pathways (plural) in anticipation of issues that we must overcome.

The translation of the inspirational plan of the superintendent through formal and informal communication must be both persistent and consistent. Both the vision and the urgency must be communicated clearly and simply.

Nancy Duarte believes that the most memorable presentations contain a balance of ethical appeal, logical appeal, and emotional appeal:

> Stating fact after fact in an hour-long presentation doesn't signal to the audience why these facts are important. Use emotions as a tool to bring emphasis to the facts so they stand out. If you don't, you're making the audience work too hard to identify the decision they are to make. Staying flat and factual might work in a scientific report but simply won't work for the oral delivery of persuasive content.[8]

And that's what you should be communicating with the inspiration . . . persuasive content.

Support

Hans, Annamarie, and Jennifer Bleiker are experts in citizen participation. Their *Citizen Participation Handbook* is full of ideas for developing what they term "informed consent" among potentially affected interests, accumulated over many years of work with government agencies. One entry in the handbook lists some of the possible objectives:

- Legitimizing your agency, project, or process, and maintaining that legitimacy;
- Establishing or maintaining the legitimacy of earlier decisions or assumptions;
- Getting to know all of the potentially affected interests;
- Seeing the project from the stakeholders' perspective;
- Identifying/understanding common problems;
- Generating alternative solutions;
- Clarifying key issues;
- Protecting and enhancing credibility;
- Verifying information is communicated, received, and understood by the potentially affected interests;
- Receiving and understanding all of the information communicated to you; and
- Depolarizing those who have diametrically opposed values or that are polarized for some other reason. [9]

Depending upon the local conditions, most or all of these might be valid reasons for informing or including your stakeholders. Clearly, a meeting to enlist ideas will involve a different approach from a meeting to share information. Decide intent and purpose before developing any presentation or scheduling any meetings.

Scope

The scope of the vision must be the broad spectrum of the entire district. Implementation can be phased, but everyone must understand that eventually this will be "the way we do things around here."

Creating successful islands of innovation that are aimed at high achievers who will succeed regardless is not the point. Characterization of this as a "pilot project" or "something we are going to try" may create pockets of innovation and excellence but will not take performance-based education to scale within the entire district.

Strategy and Reach

The inspiration is best conveyed through stories that illustrate the vision. Celebrate those who understand the vision of performance-based learning by sharing their stories. The best way to hear and see these stories is conversational intimacy.

Boris Groysberg and Michael Slind say, "For leaders the pursuit of intimacy in communication means stepping down from their corporate perch and then stepping up to the challenge of speaking with employees in ways that are personal, authentic, and transparent. It's partly a matter of style and partly a state of mind."[10] These are conversations that involve *listening for learning, not listening to respond.*

The reach has got to be deep and wide. Everyone in the organization must understand what the superintendent wants to do and why. This means getting the superintendent and the employees into situations where the conversation can be less formal and more personal. This is a message that is not delivered behind a podium, but in everyday conversation. This is time-consuming, but necessary since it is less effective to have the inspiration delivered by a "spokesperson" second- or thirdhand.

Timing

A perceptive superintendent is aware that there are inflection points in the life of the district. Capitalizing on these windows of opportunity is critical to the success of this innovative change. Clearly, the change from traditional programming to performance-based is not as simple as flipping a switch. But with the appropriate groundwork, creating the educational environment in which each student can reach their potential through a version of performance-based education is feasible even in the largest of districts.

Continuum

This is a substantial change to the way the district educates. It requires a continuous flow of professional development to staff. It requires a change in mindset among district leaders. Without a leadership pipeline, the change to performance-based education will not be sustainable.

Turnover is an issue that must be addressed in the transition. When asked, most newly hired superintendents will say they intend to stay in the district long term. And yet, the average tenure of a superintendent is about three years.

New leadership after the conversion to performance-based education should come from within the district. This increases the chances that the system will remain intact. It is natural for a new hire to want to change things. External candidates, despite professed support for performance-based learning, will lack an understanding of the system and will tend to want to change critical components of the system, with the unintended consequence of making it less effective.

Staffing

Obviously, that there may be some losses during the transition to performance-based education. The more the inspirational message can connect educators to the reasons they became teachers, the more successful you will be in retaining existing staff.

As mentioned earlier, the national statistics on teacher retention are horrible to begin with. By year five, half of teachers leave the profession, and another group leaves teaching for administration. [11]

Performance-based education will address some, but not all, of the frustrations that these professionals face. Teaching in a district that encourages innovation and collaboration is exciting and rewarding. Practitioners of performance-based education are given the opportunity to attain mastery, the autonomy to do what works for their students, and the purpose of ultimate student success—the three key motivators. [12]

Assessment and Analysis

How do you know that message has been received? There are many tools for assessing the climate and attitudes of the district. Both formal and informal surveys should be used to assess the effectiveness of the message. Frequency is critical. An annual survey at the end of the school year is not sufficient.

You can now check on employee engagement on a weekly basis. A new software package allows staff to check in regularly. It is called *People-Spark*. [13] Employees spend ten minutes at the end of each week answering a few simple questions. The results are put into a dashboard that is shared with leadership. Imagine the power of a report on engagement that is delivered to the superintendent on a weekly basis!

Logistics

The inspiration delivery must play to the strengths of the leader. If the superintendent's forte is a one-on-one conversation, then small group discussions about the vision might be more appropriate than large gatherings. If the superintendent is a strong and passionate public speaker, then community forums and town hall meetings might play better to their strengths. Use the tools with which leadership is comfortable; don't try to create new ones.

Mistakes

Inspiration that is too specific is confining, not visionary. There needs to be enough room within your statements of vision to accommodate all sorts of actions and interpretations and to measure those actions against several simple statements of value. This is a call to action, not a to-do list.

Some Points to Remember about Inspiration

- Inspiration comes from the top of the hierarchy. It is the responsibility of the district superintendent, but is not sole-sourced. Summarize the vision of the future in a few simple sentences.

- Visionary leadership comes from listening well. Persuasive content comes from a balance of emotional, ethical, and logical appeals.
- Inspiration for change comes from repetition, content, style, enthusiasm, and the absence of outside distractions. Inspiration conveys hope for the future.
- Include stakeholders in the inspiration. Decide what is needed from them, participation or agreement, and plan the meetings accordingly.
- The conversion to performance-based teaching and learning is not a pilot project and should not be described as such. The reach should be extensive. Everyone in the organization should understand that this is personal for the superintendent.
- Capitalize on inflection points to lay the groundwork for this conversion.
- Identify an in-house succession pipeline in order to sustain the change.
- Check in frequently with staff to measure engagement.
- Inspiration delivery must play to the strengths of the leadership.

NOTES

1. Llopis, Glenn. "10 Ways to Inspire Your Team." *Forbes* 193(5), 2013.

2. "But They Did Not Give Up." The University of Kentucky. n.d. http://www.uky.edu/~eushe2/Pajares/OnFailingG.html (accessed November 28, 2015).

3. Hendry, Eric. "7 Epic Fails Brought to You By the Genius Mind of Thomas Edison." Smithsonian.com. November 20, 2013. http://www.smithsonianmag.com/innovation/7-epic-fails-brought-to-you-by-the-genius-mind-of-thomas-edison-180947786/?all (accessed November 28, 2015).

4. Couros, George. "Why We Don't Truly Embrace Failure." *The Principal of Change.* September 14, 2014. http://georgecouros.ca/blog/archives/4769 (accessed November 28, 2015).

5. Badash, Yovell. *No Child Held Back: Creating a New Vision for Education Reform in the 21st Century.* New York: Yovell Badash, 2013.

6. Jellison, Jerald. *Managing the Dynamics of Change.* New York: McGraw-Hill, 2006.

7. Lopez, Shane J. *Making Hope Happen.* New York: Atria Books. 2013.

8. Duarte, Nancy. *Resonate.* Hoboken, NJ: John Wiley and Sons, 2010.

9. Bleiker, Hans, Annamarie Bleiker, and Jennifer Bleiker. *Citizen Participation Handbook.* Monterey: Institute for Participatory Management and Planning, 2012.

10. Groysberg, Boris, and Michael Slind. *Talk, Inc.* Boston: Harvard Business Review Press, 2012.

11. "Facts about the Teaching Profession for a National Conversation." U.S. Department of Education. 2011. www.ed.gov/documents/respect/teaching-profession-facts.doc (accessed August 14, 2015).

12. Pink, Daniel H. *Drive.* New York: Penguin, 2009.

13. PeopleSpark. 2015. http://peoplespark.com/ (accessed November 29, 2015).

Chapter Two

Leadership

There is nothing more difficult to take in hand, more perilous to conduct, or more uncertain in its success, than to take the lead in the introduction of a new order of things. For he who innovates will have for enemies all those who are well off under the existing order of things, and only lukewarm supporters in those who might be better off in the new.

—Machiavelli

For some, reordering a school or district into a system of performance-based learning methods might seem as difficult as the alchemist's dream of turning lead into gold.[1] There is no doubt that the conversion to this form of pedagogy takes a group of focused, creative professionals and a great deal of support from the board and the community.

The vision and mission of the board of supervisors or board of education must be consistent and specific. General statements such as "providing the best education available" or "every student living up to their potential" do not engender disruptive innovation. And it is only disruptive innovation that will improve proficiency beyond the current outcome plateau.

Consistency of board support is crucial, for while it is tempting for a new member or cadre of members to attempt to reshape the direction of the board in their own image, this is a disruptive and distracting practice and does not further the mission.

Boards whose proceedings are extensively reported in the media or televised have members who often succumb to the temptation to pander to their audience. This practice is often worse in communities where a position on the board is seen as a stepping-stone to a higher office.

The board should be a steadying influence on the governance over the educational organization that they serve, not a source of entertainment or embarrassment. The board should act as a team to advise, support, and defend the important work of educating the children of the community.

While it may be tempting for individuals to hold fast to their personal interpretation of how this should be accomplished, the transition to a version of performance-based education will require the board *to act as one* in support of the conversion.

Intent

Leaders have the best opportunity to influence the engagement of their colleagues by engendering hope. Without hope, there is very little employee engagement. Gallup has polled on this issue and found that 69 percent of employees who were enthusiastic (had hope) about the future, were engaged in their jobs.[2]

As mentioned earlier, Shane Lopez, in his book *Making Hope Happen*, is very specific about the elements needed to engender hope. Goals, not simply wishes or daydreams, are the first requirement. The goals should be plausible, but can be unlikely. Second, to have hope, a person must also believe they have agency (i.e., the ability to make things happen). The third element necessary for someone to have hope is that they have planned multiple pathways to reach those goals:[3]

> One of the greatest challenges for leaders is to initiate new efforts that will create subsequent organizational growth. If as a leader, you are not creating hope and helping people see the way forward, chances are, no one else is either.[4]

Focused, Creative Professionals

A superintendent who orchestrates this transition from traditional pedagogy to a performance-based learning model should possess position awareness, persuasive abilities, empathy, and authenticity. A leader worried about not being in complete control should not try this.

Leadership must be distributed, and ultimately, a high-potential successor must be selected and coached. The leader of a large district is likely used to not having all the controls at their fingertips, but they will have to let go of even more, trusting their good staff members to do great things.

The stance of district leaders will probably have to change because almost everyone has a stance that does not easily support innovation. According to Roger Martin, there are two kinds of "stance." He calls our factory setting the "contented model defense"; it is the way most of us are hardwired. In the contented model defense, we adopt a theory based upon the facts as we understand them and then accumulate data that supports the theory.

Martin says, "The problem with single-mindedly seeking to justify and confirm the veracity of the existing model is that the contented model defender won't treat disconfirming data as valid, much less salient." With this stance, information that doesn't confirm the original hypothesis is dismissed. It is assumed to be either unreliable or untrue.

Alternatives have also become a problem, and not a possibility. They are to be eliminated, disproved, or shown to be wrong. Innovation under a leader with this stance is highly unlikely at best. However, there is a more productive stance. Martin calls it the "optimistic model seeker."

A leader who is an optimistic model seeker believes that the current hypothesis is the best model available, but "they are forever testing what they think they know against the best available data. Their goal is refutation of their current belief, because refutation represents not failure, but an advance."[5]

With some effort, most individuals can change their factory setting to the more adaptable optimistic model seeker. This is the stance of leaders who will be comfortable with the innovations necessary to transition to performance-based learning and distributed leadership.

In the traditional educational model, effective teaching is viewed as an activity done by those who have talent and perform in isolation. Effective teachers must be identified, hired, and retained. Those less talented are either to be tolerated or encouraged to leave. For an organization whose core mission is education, this is neither productive nor appropriate.

Raising the quality of public education will only come with changing how teachers are viewed and treated, resulting in changing what happens in the classroom. Leadership and authority must be distributed to the teachers, and with that responsibility, they can collaboratively improve the effectiveness of the entire corps.

Distributed leadership will mean that every teacher is empowered and expected to innovate in their classroom pedagogy and that work is done collaboratively. Of course, the proposed innovative practices are heavily vetted initially at the lowest level of a flattened hierarchy (the professional learning communities). The potential failures are overcome in the planning process. Once implemented, the innovative practices are continually improved until they work the way they were originally intended, or in many cases even better.

Communication

No one follows a leader they do not trust. Amy Lyman has researched leadership for over twenty years. As the cofounder of the Great Place to Work Institute, she is convinced that a trustworthy leader creates the environment that moves an organization toward excellence. In her book, *The Trustworthy*

Leader, she discusses the six distinct elements of a trustworthy leader: honor, inclusion, engaging followers, sharing information, developing others, and moving through uncertainty.[6]

Lyman spoke to the issue of job instability in school district leadership at the 2012 Great Places to Work conference in Atlanta, Georgia. Answering a question from the audience, she said that acknowledging the basis of the job's instability is crucial to trust building.

Although a newly appointed superintendent may desire the position to be long term, and it is permissible to admit that, there are often issues that arise that may shorten his or her tenure—the will of the board of education, the desires of the community, family issues, or future opportunities to make a difference. Lyman felt it is more authentic to acknowledge this.[7]

"How long will you stay?" is often a question that is asked in the media frenzy when a new superintendent is hired. Rather than dismissing the question as inconsequential and saying that it is your intention to stay long term, it is far better to admit that there are many factors that will ultimately influence your longevity. The superintendent has control of only a few of those. It is best to recognize those issues in answering the question. This factual communication immediately begins to build credibility and trust.

Seven months into his superintendency in Oakland, Antwan Wilson began the difficult work of improving the five worst-performing schools in the district. The schools had been identified by his board prior to his appointment. He invited parents, teachers, community leaders, and charter school operators to submit their ideas for improving these schools.

As Stephen Covey says in *The 8th Habit,* leadership is a choice that you make between the stimulus and your response.[8] Facing a community outcry about inviting charter school operators to the table, Wilson's response was classic. "I'd rather be where people come in and speak passionately than someplace where you have to convince people to care. In Oakland, people do care about schools."[9]

Support

As mentioned before, district leadership must have the wholehearted support of the board in this transition. The significance and enforcement of board policy varies from district to district. However, once the decision to convert to performance-based learning is made, the unanimous passage of a zero-dropouts policy will be taken as a sign that the board strongly supports the changes the superintendent wants to make.

Board support is particularly crucial in smaller districts where many of the staff are friends and acquaintances of the board members. There will be urgent phone calls to board members about the various changes and dire predictions of the consequences. It is helpful if each board member, upon getting a call, does not waiver in their support for the superintendent and the new direction.

Scope

If you are going to distribute leadership, reciprocity is absolutely critical. Amy Lyman tells the story of her interview with Chris Van Gorder, the chief executive officer at Scripps Health. Van Gorder became the head of the organization during an extremely difficult time. Votes of no confidence for previous leaders, financial difficulties, and a toxic culture at the Scripps hospitals had resulted in stressful staffing issues. He set about to create a better culture, but he knew it wouldn't be easy.

"He described his change initiative as a systemic process in which he, as the leader who had the responsibility, resources, and power to start the process, would take the first step." His first step was to invite others into the process. Staff participation can take many forms.

Often it is simply information sharing or audience participation. Instead, Van Gorder invited the staff to not only participate, but also to make the decisions. His Leadership Academy for middle managers would meet on a monthly basis throughout the year. He announced publicly that all of its participants would be the leaders in changing the culture.

The first no-holds-barred question-and-answer session of the new Leadership Academy was a grueling two-and-a-half hours. Van Gorder answered every question that didn't violate an employee's rights or confidentiality. He even told the group he wanted them to learn how to ask tough questions, and gently chided them when he felt they weren't being tough enough on him. It was so successful that it became a part of every other annual Leadership Academy since.[10]

There are clearly differences in the levels of bureaucracy in an organization as big as Chris Van Gorder's (over sixteen thousand employees and volunteers) and many of the school districts in this country, but the actions should be similar—there must be reciprocity between the leaders and the followers.

Strategy and Reach

Gallup asked over ten million people to agree or disagree with a statement that their supervisor "seems to care about me as a person." They found that the individuals who responded positively were more likely to stay at the organization, had more engaged customers, and were more productive than those who responded negatively.[11]

While it is difficult to know thousands of employees personally, it is important for leaders to deliver positive energy and compassion. Rath and Conchie describe Mervyn Davies as an example. He was the chief executive of Standard Chartered PLC (a multinational financial services corporation) from 2001 to 2006 and was chairman of the board from 2006 to 2009. Davies said that "organizational leaders must have a 'positive bias' because employees simply 'don't want to follow negative people around.'"

In addition to being very open about his personal struggles as his wife battled breast cancer, Davies demonstrated his concern for his employees' mental and physical health by initiating several programs within the organization focusing on staff well-being. He always encouraged his direct reports to put their family first. "He knew that for people to truly love their organization, it needed to have a heart."[12]

Lyman also writes about this:

> Understanding does not come from simply hearing information or from receiving an e-mail in your inbox. There is always a necessary additional phase after the information comes in: time for questions and answers, time to ensure that people understand the information shared . . . an approach based in both the value of information and the value of people."[13]

Stephen Covey says leadership is not a position, but a choice. That choice is made between the action and the reaction. It is your choice in how to react, even though the interval may be a split second. Nevertheless, you have the choice as to how you will react to a given circumstance or action.[14]

How can you personally connect with staff in a large school district? At Charlotte-Mecklenburg Schools (at the time, the seventeenth largest district in the United States), former Superintendent Dr. Peter Gorman built into his calendar one ten-minute phone call every week with a teacher or staff member who was doing outstanding work (based on an endorsement from their supervisor). Sometimes he would call a teacher in the evening, or a bus driver on her lunch break.

Of course, the staff research to get the superintendent enough information for the call took much longer than the call itself, but all who participated (including Dr. Gorman) agreed it was worthwhile. He said that sometimes the most difficult part of the conversation was convincing the person he called that he was really the superintendent and not some prankster pulling a practical joke!

Timing

Superintendents new to the job have the advantage of a "honeymoon" (typically a six-month to nine-month period of benign neglect in which the board, the media, and the community let the superintendent do and say just about anything that is justifiable). But what if you decide to eliminate the dropouts and transition to a performance-based innovative system within your district and your honeymoon is over?

At the Annapolis Sailing School, instructors take the brand new sailors out on the Chesapeake Bay in a *Rainbow*. This is a beginner's boat that has so much weight on the deep keel that it is almost impossible to tip it over even in a heavy crosswind. Wind direction is the key to sailing well, and one of the best indicators of wind direction are the telltales, small ribbons attached to the rigging.

Many superintendents become very sensitive to inflection points in the ebb and flow of board and community support. These are the telltales of leadership. Take advantage of those points of inflection. Reading these will be necessary to create a sense of urgency. Begin discussions about improvement. How do we keep all of our students in school so that we can teach them? How do we give them the best educational environment in which to learn?

Continuum

Leaders must provide a buffer from unnecessary upheaval and a clear vision of what is expected. The longer the tenure, the better the buffer. Waters and Marzano say, "The positive correlation between superintendent length of service and student achievement affirms the value of leadership stability and of a superintendent remaining in a district long enough to see the positive impact of his or her leadership on student learning and achievement."[15]

But as discussed earlier, stability in leadership, especially in education organizations, is a dream rarely fulfilled. What is worse, in a tragic copy of similar business practice, the next individual in an educational leadership position feels duty bound to change whatever was done by his or her predecessor, just to prove their worthiness for the position. There are some notable exceptions to this practice, but their work is often obscured by the continuous upward personnel churn of most K–12 education institutions.

Stability in leadership starts at the dais in the boardroom. Since the majority of school supervisory boards are elected, it is not surprising that membership changes over time. Nevertheless a system of governance transition that provides consistency is critical to continuous improvement. It is difficult, if not impossible, to enlist followers to a cause associated with leadership (whether the superintendent or the board) that is short term, unless program consistency is assured through a formal transition process or board policy and governance.

For the freedom to make progress, superintendents and their executive teams should also have some stability. Boards should consider discussing contract renewal terms at least twelve months in advance. This gives everyone an opportunity to make plans and either exit gracefully or get busy.

Staffing

Gallup found that members of strong teams are as committed to their personal lives as they are to their work. The most productive team members work hard and play hard, always having enough time to do what is important with their families as well as being devoted and passionate about the work they do.

They also found that the most successful teams embraced diversity. "Having a team composed of individuals who look at issues similarly, who have been the product of comparable educational backgrounds, and who have experiences with similar track records and approaches is not a sound basis for success."[16]

But where do you find a diverse pool of candidates? The Gallup research states that strong teams are actually a talent magnet. Top talent seeks out strong teams because that's where the work gets done.

Healthy debate with attention to results is another characteristic of a strong team. Because they are all focused on and agree about what they believe is best for the organization, they can argue and even strenuously disagree. But in the end, the team gains strength and cohesion from disagreement. Coincidently, failing teams tend to personalize disagreements, which spiral into territorial divisions.

Assessment and Analysis

Whether your district is large or small, you must combine individual strengths to give the team leadership leverage. Tom Rath and Barry Conchie contradict the myth of the well-rounded leader who is not only competent but also above average in each and every leadership skill. "If you spend your life trying to be good at everything, you will never be great at anything. While our society encourages us to be well-rounded, this approach inadvertently leads to mediocrity."[17]

They categorize thirty-four strengths into four domains of leadership: executing, influencing, relationship building, and strategic thinking. Each of these thirty-four strengths has a nuanced relationship to the four domains. Their theory is that no one can possibly be equally strong in all of these areas, but a diverse leadership team might provide a balance of strengths in each of the domains.

Their organization's research (Gallup) has found that high-performing teams tend to have several things in common. One aspect of high-performing teams is agreement among the members about the goals and priorities of the organization. Members of the team make decisions based upon what is best for the organization and not based upon personal preference.

Frequent assessment of your team's progress is one way to continue to progress. In order to be productive, those assessments must be electronic, easy to analyze, anonymous, and actionable.

Logistics

Believe it or not, there are also three potentially negative issues to having no dropouts that as a leader you must be prepared to address: some of those students do not score well on common assessments, some of those students have discipline issues, and keeping more students in school often creates school capacity problems.

Students who drop out are often not in the highest percentiles on common assessments. In a universe obsessed with gauging the quality of an educational environment by its test scores on three to five "core" subjects, keeping each and every student in school means that, at least initially, those scores could be lower. And since many states grade schools and districts based upon common assessments, that means lower grades for schools and districts in the short run.

The second issue is that some students drop out of school because they have been the source of school discipline problems. Once these students drop out, there is a perverse incentive for administrators not to try too hard to get them to return. A district that wants to increase its graduation rate and take its dropout rate to zero must also be prepared to address the issues that caused these students to become discipline problems. This may call for adjustments in staffing or assignments to accommodate these issues.

The third unintended consequence of zero dropouts is potential overcrowding at the high schools. Typically, junior and senior enrollments at the high schools are lower than the number of freshman and sophomores.

If the cohort graduation rate (the calculation of the percentage of freshman that graduate in four years) is currently at the national average of 81 percent, and a zero dropout rate is put into place, the high school capacity may need to be increased by as much as 19 percent. Every two-thousand-student high school will now be required to accommodate 2,380 students. Some adjustment in capacity can be accomplished by "floating" teachers. However, this is not the best for effective classroom practices.

For most districts, the initial drop in average test scores and the need for additional capacity are counterbalanced by the benefit of having all of their students graduate. Almost every administrative decision in education comes with unintended consequences. Knowing what some of the unintended consequences will be may help you prepare and address them appropriately.

Whether you are a superintendent, a board member, an administrator, a teacher, or a parent, the benefits of performance-based education are real. While the vision must be formed and communicated by leadership, some of the best ideas might come from sources outside your own experience that may not be in the organizational hierarchy at all—news stories, interviews, maybe even books!

Mistakes

There are many experiences that serve to build a leader's abilities. Chris Van Gorder was a lowly security guard at a hospital complex (not Scripps) to support himself through school. He was doing his rounds in the basement hallway in the middle of the night, and he recognized the hospital's chief administrator walking toward him, coming from a late-night meeting. He says, "He walked by me as if I didn't exist." Van Gorder was crushed. He still remembers that encounter. It has influenced his leadership style. He has incorporated reciprocity into every interaction with his staff and volunteers and has made Scripps a leader in the health-care industry.[18]

Some Points to Remember about Leadership

- Strong board support is critical to the success of the transition to a performance-based system of innovation.
- Distribute leadership for collaboration. Reciprocity is a necessary element of distributed leadership.
- Leaders promote innovation by changing their personal stance to an optimistic model seeker from a contented model defender.
- Create hope to increase engagement.
- A successful leadership team will have diverse backgrounds and experiences and complementary strengths.
- Zero dropouts comes with unintended consequences. Some of those students do not score well on common assessments, some of those students have discipline issues, and keeping more students in school often creates additional school capacity needs.

NOTES

1. Matson, John. "Fact or Fiction?: Lead Can Be Turned into Gold." *Scientific American*, January 31, 2014.

2. Rath, Tom, and Barry Conchie. *Strengths-Based Leadership.* New York: Gallup Publishing, 2008.

3. Lopez, Shane J. *Making Hope Happen.* New York: Atria Books, 2013.

4. Rath and Conchie, *Strengths-Based Leadership.*

5. Martin, Roger. *The Opposable Mind.* Boston: Harvard Business School Publishing, 2009.

6. Lyman, Amy. *The Trustworthy Leader.* San Francisco: Jossey-Bass, 2012.

7. Lyman, Amy, remarks in response to a question by Michael K. Raible. Presentation at the Great Places to Work conference: The Trustworthy Leader (September 2012).

8. Covey, Stephen R. *The 8th Habit: From Effectiveness to Greatness.* New York: Free Press, 2004.

9. Payton, Brenda. "Oakland's New Schools Superintendent Confronts the C-word." *San Francisco Chronicle*, February 27, 2015.

10. Lyman, *The Trustworthy Leader.*

11. Rath, and Conchie, *Strengths-Based Leadership.*

12. Ibid.

13. Lyman, *The Trustworthy Leader.*

14. Covey, *The 8th Habit.*

15. Waters, J. Timothy, and Robert J. Marzano. *The Primacy of Superintendent Leadership.* Denver: McRel, 2008.

16. Rath, and Conchie, *Strengths-Based Leadership.*

17. Ibid.

18. Lyman, *The Trustworthy Leader.*

Chapter Three

Perspiration

I experience more failure every five minutes of teaching than I experienced in a whole week as an engineer. Giving a presentation to NASA about how the thermal protection system of a spacecraft is connected to its primary structure is a cakewalk compared to getting 30 teenagers excited about logarithms.

—Ryan Fuller, a former aerospace engineer who now teaches[1]

The implementation of a version of performance-based education program is a heavy lift. District leaders who tour a successful school district in the hope of finding their "secret sauce," often go away discouraged. There is a lot of hard work involved.

Intent

Quick wins for students ultimately turn into positive academic momentum. That positive momentum is what propels students toward continued progress in performance-based learning. Just as in football, it is the well-placed block on a defensive lineman that creates the opportunity for a running back to gain a few more yards, so it is with education.

The educational and administrative staff will spend much of their time removing the barriers to learning so that students can begin to achieve the academic momentum that will propel them to the next level. What is the payoff for all this hard work? The reward is seeing students who are successful, not just in their time in school in the district, but in life.

Practice

For example, keeping every student in school means every teacher and multiple administrators are busy throughout the school year. Even though some states now require students to stay in school until they are eighteen years old, there are still some students on the first days of school that the director of pupil personnel has to find and get back into school. If they miss too much, it might mean they must be enrolled in a virtual program to catch up, and that means the virtual program staff and the dropout prevention specialist are mobilized to find out not only where to place the students and which classes to enroll them in, but also what the student is interested in and why they did not initially come to school.

Transfer students from other districts also pose problems. These students require a schedule of courses and a collaborative effort of teachers, counselors, the virtual program staff, and school administrators. Each student's skills and proficiencies need to be assessed so that an individualized and multitiered program to address the deficiencies can be created, and these students can graduate with a high school diploma.

Though many legislators don't seem to be aware of it, teaching is hard work. Half of the new teachers in the United States leave the profession in the first five years. Sometimes the survivors say that the longer you stay, the easier it gets, but not always. "In teaching, a person can be extremely competent, work relentlessly, and still fail miserably. Especially in the first year or two on the job, success can seem impossible," says Ryan Fuller.[2]

In a performance-based classroom, those unfamiliar with data analysis must become familiar with that aspect of the program. Veteran teachers uneasy with technology in the classroom need to become adept at incorporating the new tools into their pedagogy.

In order to ease the transition into performance-based education, you may want to give your teachers the option of continuing to teach with the traditional methodology. But there should be little choice about the use of technology.

Consider implementing a one-to-one technology initiative and a bring-your-own-device protocol for all students. This will require technical support from the members of your staff that are familiar with instructional technology.

Instructional technology support for the teachers is only as good as the hardware and software support supplied by the IT department. The mindset of this department should be educational, not technical. They should understand that if a teacher cannot access the features of the system, the device is useless.

Visits to every classroom should be weekly and at random so that teachers are not able to prepare several engaging lessons for a scheduled evaluation. Every lesson should be engaging. Reviews should be informal with nothing written down. This is not punitive. But the implications are understood. Specific teachers may require help and should receive it without stigma, if needed.

The rule that no child fails requires constant attention from the educators. Remediation is given immediately to students who are struggling—before they fail. And multilayered interventions are put into place for those who continue to struggle. Students still must deal with life's issues—extreme poverty, drug and alcohol abuse, dysfunctional families, and juvenile detention. However, staff awareness of these issues is not sufficient; staff interventions are required so that these students are not lost. Teams made up of administrators, counselors, and the dropout prevention specialist should address these challenges in a timely fashion with each student individually.

Personalized learning plans need to be prepared and documented for every student. Again, administrators and counselors are involved in developing a plan that addresses each student's needs and career aspirations. This also means that no student is held back by virtue of their age. For staff, that means there may be a new student showing up in your classroom at any time during the year. Accelerated learning is hard work, too.

Leaders

The district leadership must model the organization's values. This cannot be an executive staff that checks out at the end of the school year and checks back in a couple of weeks before school starts. There are many districts in which even the executive staff is not engaged full time in the summer.

So how do some leaders create an organizational atmosphere in which everyone is willing to work hard, and other leaders generate a compliance mindset instead? Jeff Haden wrote a column in *Inc.* magazine in which he identified eight characteristics of outstanding leaders. "Set the example," he explains. "Employees notice what you do. When you're in charge, everyone watches what you do. The difference lies in how you do what you do . . . and what that says about you."[3]

Many professions these days have peaks and valleys. There are times when the work is frenetic and others when a long lunch is acceptable. When deadlines approach and it seems everyone on staff is working extended hours, some leaders will order dinner in for the entire office and manage the work by walking around to each work station, answering questions and providing encouragement to the staff. Others will offer heartfelt appreciation for all the hard work being done, as they leave the office at their usual time, indicating they know the project is in good hands.

These are two entirely different approaches to virtually the same situation. Whose staff do you think gets the most productive work done?

Communication

An employee who feels respected and appreciated accomplishes far more than an employee who is working for a paycheck. The messaging around the transition to performance-based education must convey that respect and appreciation.

This message is best conveyed in person. A general e-mail blast saying "thank you for all your hard work" is far less effective than a one-to-one thank-you from the boss. It may feel as though you can do without food and water for days if the superintendent stops by your classroom to say thanks for putting in those extra hours!

Although the conversion to performance-based learning involves a great deal of difficult work, the purpose of the work goes to the heart of why most educators picked this as a career. The communication focus must be on why the work is important and on celebrating the hard work and accomplishments of students.

Support

Knowing that all of the staff members are going to be overextended in many cases without additional compensation during the transition, this is the time to focus the support of your community. Gestures of support from parents and local business partners to demonstrate how much the staff is appreciated are especially welcome during the first years of transition.

Scope

If there is one particular school feeder system that will benefit from the switch to performance-based learning more than the others, it may work to use it as a model. However, it is important to identify this as the first phase of a project that will ultimately be district-wide, for two reasons. First, this is not a methodology that lends itself to an isolated experiment. Second, it is always more difficult to try something new and break a sweat if your peers continue to work at their traditional methodology and pace.

Those excited about the new direction will share their enthusiasm; those who struggle will share their pain. There is an old sales maxim that says a satisfied customer will recommend the product to four other people, while a dissatisfied customer will complain to twelve others.

Strategy and Reach

The strategy must be one of reciprocity. What responsibilities can be removed from the teaching staff as they take on the transition to performance-based learning? Are there chances to use the tools of technology, student assistants, or parent volunteers to help staff accomplish some of their already substantial workload?

Timing

There is no perfect way to begin hard work. Some find it is best to start slowly and gradually build in intensity. Others find that "just doing it" is better than pacing. In any case, one must be prepared mentally to accomplish the work, and that comes from the inspiration in the previous chapter. There is nothing more difficult than hard work that you do not want to do. Make the work easier by praising accomplishments and randomly rewarding progress.

Continuum

The work of transition is ongoing. Your staff will continue to work hard to make it happen and make it better. Innovative educational practice is not a destination, but an ongoing collaborative journey.

Staffing

Everyone you interview will tell you they have a strong work ethic. So how can you determine if a candidate is a hard worker? Changing interview questions from the usual questions can help:

- Tell me about a time when you . . .
- What will your references tell me about your work ethic?
- If you were able to retire right now, would you? And what would you do?
- How did you fund your college education?
- When was your first paying job?
- What are you currently reading?
- What did you do to prepare for this interview, and what did you find out about us?

Assessment and Analysis

Educators usually spend a significant amount of time doing their job. A simple measurement of time spent is not a good indicator of whether or not an individual is working hard. Colleagues in a collaborative environment like performance-based education can generally identify those individuals who are "coasting."

An informal 360-degree review is one of the best ways to identify a team member who is not up to standard. Clearly, evidence of work product and progress is another means of determining an individual's dedication to the work. Unfortunately, the data and analysis on this aspect of the work tends to be very subjective.

Beware of personal biases, as they can easily influence subjective analysis. If you are an early riser and tend to arrive at work before anyone else, your bias will cause you to see someone who arrives late as less than optimal, even if they stay late to work after you leave.

Susan Cain writes about the struggles at the Harvard Business School, an institution that assumes it is training future CEOs. Students are measured by their participation in class in Harvard's traditional case study format. Trouble is, those that tend to participate are the extroverts—more vocal, verbal thinkers. The introverts are left in the dust, even though their ideas may be as good or even better than those who dominate the conversation. [4]

Logistics

Reciprocity is a necessity for any difficult task. There may be teachers who request additional tools like voice reinforcement to help them with their jobs. Others may decide that another tool will help them, and every effort should be made to give them that tool if they request it.

Basic technology is just about the only teaching tool that should not be optional. Every classroom should have an interactive whiteboard and every student should have access to at least one electronic device.

A collaborative and participatory environment is also a key to motivating everyone to work hard. It is not east to sit and watch from the sidelines when everyone else is participating. Although many of the classroom doors will be closed because the noise level tends to be higher, there should be very little classroom isolation. The frequent conversations among colleagues in the professional learning communities (PLCs) will reinforce this.

Mistakes

During a particularly stressful year that involved layoffs from budget cuts and the discussion of a pay-for-performance system of compensation for all employees, one large district put a time-clock system into place for hourly employees.

The system as installed accurately recorded each employee's arrival and departure time. The loyal hourly support staff who would normally come into work a few minutes before and work a few minutes after the official quitting time were now cautioned to refrain from that practice because the district did not want to pay for overtime.

Everything about this was wrong. Even though the installation of the time clocks had been planned for over a year, the timing of the actual installation sent a message of distrust to the hourly support staff. This was further complicated by the caution about working overtime. The loss in productivity, although never measured, was significant. Morale among the loyal hourly support staff has never recovered. The unintended consequences of a legitimate equipment installation have been an irreversible loss of productivity, trust, and employee morale.

Some Points to Remember about Hard Work

- The conversion from traditional methods to performance-based methods is hard work. The introduction of competency-based teaching and learning makes every teacher feel like a novice again. The initial years are still the hardest. Enlist the support of local businesses and the community at large for the professionals who are working so hard.
- Keeping students in school requires the diligent efforts of several staff members, particularly at the beginning of each school year. Transfer students also require additional care for proper placement and scheduling.
- Instructional and technical support is necessary for those unfamiliar with the tools, data applications, and analysis.
- Every classroom should receive a visit every week for an informal review. Review regularly, but be conscious of subjective biases.
- Remediation is also hard work.
- Individual learning plans should be developed for each student.
- Employees notice what leaders do. Model strong values.
- The educational and administrative staff should spend much of their time eliminating barriers for students.
- An engaged employee is more productive.
- This is ultimately a district-wide effort, not an isolated experiment.
- While hiring staff, structure the interview questions to identify candidates with a strong work ethic.
- Reciprocity is a necessity. Demonstrations of gratitude should be personal. Make the work easier by praising accomplishments and randomly rewarding progress.
- Beware of the unintended consequences in the timing and messaging of actions.

NOTES

1. Fuller, Ryan. "Teaching Isn't Rocket Science. It's Harder." *Slate*. December 18, 2013. http://www.slate.com/articles/life/education/2013/12/teaching_in_america_s_highest_need_communities_isn_t_rocket_science_it_s.html (accessed July 20, 2015).
2. Ibid.
3. Haden, Jeff. "8 Things Truly Outstanding Leaders Do without Thinking." *Inc.*, April 21, 2014.
4. Cain, Susan. *Quiet*. New York: Crown Publishers, 2012.

Part II

Tools

Organizational Systems to Facilitate the Transition

Chapter Four

Creative Staffing

The real role of leadership in education . . . should not be command and control. The real role of leadership is climate control, creating a climate of possibility.

—Dr. Ken Robinson

Being creative about what responsibilities are assigned to each staff member allows them to personalize their support of performance-based education more easily. Some positions are logical extensions of the work, while others are designed to satisfy specific local requirements.

Intent

Creative staffing is a means of matching the work to be done to the skills of an individual responsible for that function. If a film crew doesn't have a gaffer (head electrician) who is responsible for the electrical installation and the lighting on the set, the film will either be made poorly or not at all. At some point in the history of filmmaking, someone decided that electricity and lighting were important enough to have a staff position created for that responsibility. Likewise, in a district that has converted its programming to performance-based learning, there are jobs that must be done that may not be required in traditional program delivery. Staff assignments need to be adjusted or positions created to get this work done.

Teachers

Since classroom teachers have a relatively short career ladder, some states have created master-teacher designations that allow effective teachers to serve as instructional supervisors while still maintaining contact with the classroom.

These teachers are given roles as professional development creators and presenters, intervention specialists, instructional coaches, mentors, coordinators of comprehensive school-based student support, or peer assistance review leaders. These responsibilities keep what are perceived to be the better teachers in touch with the classroom instruction. Unfortunately, the unintended consequence of creating these positions is that their connection to students is tangential at best. If these are the good teachers, shouldn't the number of students they teach be increased?

It comes down to compensation. Whether a teacher is currently effective or marginal, the opportunity for additional salary is very limited. Some teachers can qualify for additional compensation by further training. A master's degree or National Board Certification means an increase in many jurisdictions. In some states, a teacher receives an increase in salary for every year they are in the system, although the number of states that continue this practice is dwindling.

Other than these options, the only way for a teacher to remain in education and be assured of receiving additional future compensation is to pursue a promotion to administration. Today's administrative ranks are filled with professionals with only a few years in the classroom.

The master-teacher system delays some qualified professionals from seeking promotion to administrative positions, but for others it is simply another rung on the career ladder that culminates in a higher paying administrative position. Of the 3.4 million teachers in the 2011–2012 school year, only 57.7 percent had more than nine years of teaching experience.[1] History also tells us that almost half of novice teachers will leave the profession within five years.

Keeping, supporting, and continuing to provide targeted training to teachers is far less disruptive and far more efficient than continuing to take on board more novices every year. If we are to get serious about solving our shortage of teachers, there are a number of things we can do:

- We must create a career ladder for teachers that allows our most proficient classroom educators to remain in contact with the greatest number of students while making an increasingly higher salary.
- Most administrative positions should have revolving responsibilities so that seasoned veteran educators can return to teaching without penalty, and committed educators will be less inclined to seek administrative positions simply to improve their compensation.
- We must create formal programs that retain and support our novice teachers—mentorships, clerical support, pairing veteran and novice teachers, reduced contact hours, and increased professional development.

- We must make teachers' wages competitive. Since 1990, the average teacher salary, when adjusted for inflation, has decreased by 1 percent.[2]
- Consider creating a professional learning community for all of your new teachers in each school. Sharing the joys and frustrations of a new instructional environment can be therapeutic.

Other positions can help you transition to a version of performance-based learning as well.

Students

Be creative about the use of students to accomplish tasks within the district. To encourage interest in the teaching profession, allow them to serve as teacher's assistants. To encourage an interest in technology, allow students to support hardware and software. Be clear about your purpose, and align programs with that purpose. There is more detail about programs in later chapters.

Marketing Directors

The marketing directors are the district's sales force. Why does the district need sales? No matter how the district delivers its programs, whether traditionally or innovatively, there is rarely enough revenue to support what needs to be done. Using the district's nonprofit status, the marketing directors can lead an effort to encourage and ultimately gain that support.

In the conversion to performance-based education, some of the district activities are outside the norm of standard educational expenditures (e.g., an academic pep rally prior to state testing at the end of the year). The marketing directors can find financing for these activities as well as identify sources among the local businesses for in-kind donations for raffles or giveaways.

If the district has the opportunity to sell naming rights for various components of the school facilities, the marketing directors can lead this effort, too. Some states require revenue generated from the transfer of property rights to be spent for specific purposes, usually capital improvements. If you decide to pursue naming rights, identify the legal requirements within your jurisdiction.

Develop a protocol for these transactions, and identify potential issues before beginning the program. Will there be certain companies or products excluded from the program? Companies that sell tobacco or alcohol products may be some to consider. Many boards already have a process in place for naming a school. Is this a logical extension of that process?

Since much of the work within the school system is enhanced through the use of volunteers, the marketing directors can also assist with finding volunteers, screening them, and identifying the work that can be done at each school. The companies with which they are building relationships are often the source of substantial numbers of volunteers as are local centers of worship.

Technology Integration Specialists

We have not yet reached the point at which every teacher is comfortable integrating technology into their classroom experience. Changing the method of program delivery from traditional to a version of performance-based complicates the issue even further. The integration specialists can ease this transition.

When the program delivery is flipped or self-paced, these specialists can help with everything from videotaping lessons to developing exercises for individual or small-group work. Their familiarity with available software can make the conversion much less painful.

Virtual-Program Teachers

The virtual program provides the flexibility you will need to accommodate the needs of students who are struggling. They could be having issues with attending class and earning a living. They might be having trouble with a specific subject. They could simply prefer to take courses online rather than sit in a classroom. The virtual-program teachers are the key to making this work for those students.

While some students will work from home on virtual classes, the vast majority become far too distracted outside of an educational environment. This is where your computer labs can be put to use. The success rates are much higher for students with a coach or advisor available to answer questions. Having content experts available during times when a specific virtual content is being taught is even better.

College and Career Readiness Coordinator

Since much of the focus today is on career and college readiness, many districts have created a position to monitor their students' progress. The hiring of this position is only the start. The second step in the process is to develop a concise definition of what career and college readiness is. Some use a cut score on an exam like the ACT. Others require certifications.

This position can also follow students' progress once they graduate from high school, resulting in a reduced number of students having to take remedial classes in college or lacking the appropriate skills to be successful in their career.

Unfortunately there are very few leading indicators for college and career readiness. It is usually a matter of adjusting curriculum after the fact. The data received corresponds to students that the district no longer teaches. This is not to say the data should not be gathered, just that there is a lag of several years between what is being taught and the ability to identify its effectiveness.

Dropout Preventer

While most districts probably have a position or several positions similar to dropout preventer, the work in this case is more critical. This individual is the last line of defense between success and failure for many students.

If zero dropouts is the goal, the dropout preventer must have a perfect record. This position must have access to a broad range of tools and unconditional support.

Response to Intervention Teachers

One of the other keys to student success is just-in-time remediation. Wait and see is not an option. In thirteen years of school under a wait-and-see protocol, a student has 26 opportunities to succeed or fail. Under a just-in-time remediation system, that same student has 180 days and 13 years or a total of 2,340 opportunities to succeed or fail.

Once a learning deficit is identified, the first responders are the classroom teachers. But in the event that the deficit is more serious, a multilayered system of intervention is brought to bear. The teachers within this system are able to address the issues that are causing a student to struggle and get them back on grade level. The RtI (response to intervention) teachers should be accelerated recovery experts.

Project Manager

A transition of the magnitude of traditional methodology to performance based requires a full-time manager. The ideal candidate is an individual who has education experience and is a project management professional. But that person may be difficult to find. In an either/or situation, opt for the project management expertise.

Ombudsman

Unfortunately, a district is only as good as its community thinks it is. If the district's reputation is that it does not respond appropriately to student and/or parent requests, it is not effective. As a result, several large districts have considered creating the position of ombudsman to represent the needs of the students and parents within the system.

The legal aspects of a student/parent advocate who is a member of staff may be complex. Be sure to include legal counsel in the decision to create an ombudsman position.

Communication Specialist/Community Liaison for the Board

Constituent response is an important, yet time-consuming, part of being a member of the board. In addition to that aspect of service, the board often needs to be proactive with regard to issues they are considering or in seeking public input.

Consider creating a communications position that reports to the board for this purpose. This individual would clearly have to work in concert with district staff on mutual communication but might also serve to better represent the board's position to the community.

Other Possibilities

This was certainly not an all-encompassing list of the possible positions. Every local condition is nuanced and so requires variations in the work that needs to be done. The point is to not be limited by the traditional job descriptions or titles. As an organization whose budget is roughly 85 percent staff-related expenditures, you should verify that the positions you create align to the work that needs to be accomplished and proceed accordingly.

Creative staffing also means the elimination of legacy positions. In many cases, this will be the only way to make room for the new positions you create.

Leaders

The issue of creative staffing for leadership has two distinct aspects: How do you distribute staff assignments in a way that creates enough flexibility for existing or new staff to take on additional challenges, and how do you decide on the best candidate to hire?

The first aspect relates to prioritization of position assignments. Matthew May, in his book *The Laws of Subtraction* says that what you choose not to do may be more important than what you decide to do. "At the heart of every difficult decision lie three tough choices: What to pursue versus what to ignore. What to leave in versus what to leave out. What to do versus what to don't." He believes that the second part of those decisions, that is, what to ignore or leave out, may in fact be more important than the others. [3]

The world of education is perpetually resource limited. If you want to repurpose staff, you will have to prioritize assignments. This should be an exercise in subtraction as well as addition. Of course, almost every job description contains the ubiquitous "other duties as assigned" terminology, and you can probably adjust responsibilities temporarily under that provision. In the long term, you will need to formally designate who is assigned to which tasks. Since you are probably in a zero-sum environment, you will need to use subtraction to do this.

Process analysis is one way to decide which duties (that are less important) to subtract and which to add to those that satisfy a specific need. In a matrix, arrange the needs in a column down the left side of the matrix. Assign weights to each of those needs from one (the least important) to ten (the most important). List positions in rows across the top of the matrix. Identify in the boxes in the intersections how a specific position will satisfy the needs. The exercise and the weights will help you to decide position assignments, and perhaps which positions are redundant.[4]

It is tempting to adjust job descriptions to the talents of incumbents. But it is not a good long-term strategy. Adjust the position assignments to the work (the needs) to be accomplished. If the incumbent does not have the skills, train them. A position is sometimes eliminated or retitled during a reorganization. The incumbent is then given the opportunity to apply for the "new" position. Care should be taken to use this mechanism sparingly, if at all. Staff members often interpret this negatively. Trust and culture may suffer as a result.

The second aspect of leadership for creative staffing is the ability to hire the right person for a vacancy. Jeffrey Cohn and Jay Moran advise organizations on how to hire good leaders. They say there are seven attributes to look for in a candidate: integrity, empathy, emotional intelligence, vision, judgment, courage, and passion.

They suggest methods of questioning during the interview that identify these attributes:

- A case study with an ethical dilemma, but no obvious answer;
- Roleplay that involves difficult interpersonal dynamics;
- A two-step question-and-answer case study that gives a candidate the chance to change their answer;
- An opportunity for the candidate to tell about a time when they were able to imagine a solution when others reached a dead end;
- A real-life problem that they could have to solve in their new position;
- A case study that requires the candidate to demonstrate a reliable moral compass; and
- A question to determine the candidate's passion for the work.[5]

These are obviously not your average interview questions, and that's the point. In order to discover the key attributes, you have to ask and/or do the unexpected when interviewing a prospective candidate.

Communication

Safety is always important in a creative environment. Playing musical chairs with positions and responsibilities will destroy the environment that allows the innovation to occur. Communication surrounding new positions or reconfigured ones should be early, specific, and transparent. "I'm thinking of reassigning your responsibilities" isn't helpful, or reassuring. Incumbents should know their status before anything is announced publicly. The logic behind the adjustments should be clearly explained.

Support

Seek funding for positions through grant applications and/or local corporate support. If a community member suggests the need for a position, ask them if they would help build a case for funding. Sometimes an influential community partner is more successful or provides more leverage in seeking a contribution.

Be clear to the incumbent in a position that is grant funded or supported by a corporation as to what will be done when the funding is no longer available. Three to five years seems a long time at the beginning, but it goes by very quickly. There is nothing worse than an incumbent who does not know if they will have a job the next year. Wouldn't that affect your performance?

Scope

The success of your program is highly dependent upon created positions and reassigned responsibilities. Recognize staff contributions in your public presentations. The scope of these positions may be highly specialized, but their effect upon the work of the district is tangible and invaluable.

Strategy and Reach

Find a balance between the work that *needs to be done* and the work that *should be done*. Covey's four-square matrix for urgency and importance is useful here.[6] Identify those activities that are on the important side of the squares, whether they are urgent or latent. Connect a staff member to each one of these activities. If there is no one to assign, think about creating a position. If there is someone without a task on the important side of the matrix, either consider additional important assignments or eliminate the position.

Timing

Creating positions does not have to correspond to the timing of a reporting structure adjustment, but depending upon the positions created, it will tend to steer the design of the hierarchy (because you will not only be creating positions but designating a reporting structure as well).

Continuum

Although most individuals in administrative positions in education do not stay in those positions for very long, they like to know that there is some permanence to their situation. If there is no assurance to give on this score, then be upfront about it. It is a time-bound position. If the time is limited, consider using consultants or another labor force for the task instead of hiring a full-time employee.

Staffing

The position title should indicate the level of responsibility. Work with your human resources staff to determine the appropriate titles. In most districts, a title usually connects the position to a salary range.

You may be hiring individuals with credentials with which you are unfamiliar, and many people have expertise that may not be obvious on a résumé. First, hire for attitude, not skills. Second, depending upon the job, a background in education may not be required. Third, rely upon community partners that hire positions with similar requirements to advise and/or sit in on the interviews. For example, if you decide that an individual with public relations credentials is critical to your mission, work with a local advertising agency to review résumés and separate the better qualified from the marginally qualified candidates.

The tendency when hiring is to hire the best résumé—someone who has done the job before, has a degree from a prestigious university, and/or has stayed in positions for a number of years and not moved around. Regina Hartley, the human resources manager at UPS, suggests that you hire what she calls "the scrapper" over the "silver spoon," assuming they both are equally qualified.[7]

Also consider using available part-time staff where possible. Demographic studies have indicated that many of your employees will be caring for an aging parent in the next ten years. As a result, some may not be able to work full time. This is a pool of qualified individuals usually untapped by educational organizations.

Retired district personnel may also be a source of part-time assistance. Retiring staff are a significant loss of institutional knowledge. Another solution is to create an emeritus position for veteran executive staff who no longer want the long hours and pressure of a high-level position. This is often a win/win situation as it permits the district to access their expertise but takes the staff member out of "the line of fire."

Assessment and Analysis

Set expectations for the tasks to be done in the new position and monitor performance frequently. Enriched staffing is often subject to public criticism, particularly if there are no obvious results attributable to the position. Grant or corporate funders may require an analysis of results. Identify expected results and document the outcomes.

Logistics

Consider doing a simple process map for all of the important tasks with Visio or another simple software package. This will give you some idea of the responsibilities you need to assign and the tasks you will require. Now divide the tasks into rough categories based upon the necessary skills. Which incumbents have those skills? Rewrite their position descriptions.

Mistakes

Job descriptions that are too long or too specific are mistakes. Titles should be general enough to give you some flexibility in task assignments, but not so general that the new hire doesn't know what to do. This requires a delicate balance. Look at how you want to evaluate performance and build a description around that.

Some Points to Remember about Creative Staffing

- Extend the career ladder for teachers so that effective teachers can remain in contact with students without being penalized with a lack of salary.
- Keeping, supporting, and training the current teacher corps is far less expensive and disruptive than turnover. Create formal systems of support for novice teachers.
- Alignment of positions to the work required is essential to success. Consider creating positions that are aligned to performance-based learning:

  Marketing directors
  Technology integration specialists
  Virtual program teachers
  College and career readiness coordinator
  Dropout preventer
  Response to Intervention teachers
  Project manager

Ombudsman
Communication specialist/community liaison for the board

- Leaders should distribute staff assignments for flexibility and decide who best fits the requirements of the position. Explain the logic behind the reordering. Focus on creating positions for the important work, not the urgent work.
- Create temporary positions and reporting structures for tasks that require special expertise.
- Identify expected outcomes, and monitor the results for created positions. Enriched staffing is often the subject of criticism, and demonstrating results will mute it.
- All important processes should be documented with a process map.
- Don't get too specific with job descriptions. Describe what needs to be done, not how it should be done. Allow some flexibility.

NOTES

1. "Table 209.20." National Center for Education Statistics. May 2013. http://nces.ed.gov/programs/digest/d13/tables/dt13_209.20.asp (accessed November 11, 2015).

2. "National Center for Educational Statistics." Institute of Education Sciences. May 2013. http://nces.ed.gov/fastfacts/display.asp?id=28 (accessed November 11, 2015).

3. May, Matthew E. *The Laws of Subtraction*. New York: McGraw-Hill, 2013.

4. Sanderson, Rob, interview by Michael K. Raible. Vice president/operation project consultant, Bank of America (July 9, 2015).

5. Cohn, Jeffrey, and Jay Moran. *Why Are We Bad at Picking Good Leaders?* San Francisco: Jossey-Bass, 2011.

6. Covey, Stephen R. *The Seven Habits of Highly Effective People*. New York: Free Press, 1989.

7. Hartley, Regina. TED.com. October 31, 2014. https://www.ted.com/talks/regina_hartley_why_the_best_hire_might_not_have_the_perfect_resume/transcript?language=en (accessed December 10, 2015).

Chapter Five

Professional Development

He who dares to teach must never cease to learn.

—Aristotle

Although much professional development in education touts some new and improved technique and/or technology application, most is presented in a lecture format that would have been familiar to Aristotle. It is unfortunate that, regardless of the quality of the new techniques being introduced, they are often presented in a way no more exciting than a lecture with slides.

When pressed to offer something new, most presenters resort to dividing the audience into groups and then asking them to come back together and report on the group discussions. The more radical of these actually record the results on flip charts and ask the note takers to tell the reassembled audience what occurred.

Whether presenters are reading from a handwritten flip chart or from a set of bullet points projected on a screen, their summing up often consists of reading to the assembled crowd. Is it any wonder that teachers complain about the quality of their professional development?

Intent

Flipping the district by introducing a student-centered version of performance-based teaching and learning means that every teacher will need substantial professional development.

Rebecca Alber says, "Research shows that teachers tend to teach the way that they were taught. That is, of course, until we gain new insights through experience and development. And since education is always evolving, professional development is essential for teachers to enhance the knowledge and skills they need to help students succeed in the classroom."[1]

Presentations

However content is presented, the recall of the audience is subject to the Ebbinghaus Forgetting Curve. Loss of memory is exponential (80 percent in the first two days) unless reinforced through repetition of content or the use of mnemonic techniques.[2]

There are a number of presentation techniques that will improve retention. In *Beyond Bullet Points*, Cliff Atkinson takes a step-by-step approach through the process of not only improving the quality of PowerPoint presentations, but also thinking through communication with the audience.

His technique has three steps: focus, clarify, and engage. He explains that you must first distill and shape your ideas into a concise and compelling narrative. Then using a storyboard to illustrate your presentation, create a blend of message and media. Finally, increase the impact of the presentation by designing the experience for the audience, not just a read-through of the notes.[3]

Include pictures and visual metaphors in presentations. David Sibbet has been perfecting graphic facilitation for over thirty-five years. Visualization has certain properties that stimulate our awareness and thinking. Visual recording (e.g., graphic facilitation) immediately acknowledges what was heard and how it was heard. Working visually incorporates left- and right-brain thinking. Graphic displays can contain contradictory information and soften an either/or pattern of thinking about an issue.

Working with graphic metaphors (hilltops as goals, roadways as process, trees as decision devices) conveys how people are making sense of what is being discussed. Working with these metaphors opens imaginal realms. Visual arrangement helps make people aware of interrelated concepts and connections that are difficult to express with text alone.[4]

Nancy Duarte offers some tips about making your delivery memorable. She analyzes presentations graphically by using a technique called a "sparkline." The sparkline documents the flow of the presentation between what is and what could be. Modulation between these poles engages the audience. The visual record also documents time, engagement levels, and verbal cues.

Duarte argues for presentations that "tune the message" to the audience. Part of that tuning involves the use of powerful visual images as well as words that connect the audience to the message. The photo of the kid on the skateboard ready to plunge down the San Francisco hill, the image of the fishing trawler about to get swallowed by a massive wave, or the photo of a kindergartener headed to his first day of school are the kinds of "sticky" imagery Duarte is suggesting.[5]

Practice

Professional development should not just involve instructional techniques. Seth Gershenson, in an article on the Brookings Institution Brown Board, cites current research that finds that racial mismatch has a negative effect on teacher expectations. Consider incorporating "teacher training and professional development programs to routinely emphasize the importance and duty of all teachers to nurture, support, and encourage all students, regardless of their innate ability, talents, behaviors, or home circumstances."[6]

Professional development need not be delivered as a lecture. Think about other ways that the instructional staff can discuss and share successes and failures. Cheryl Boes suggests an online book club might be a way to contribute to a culture of professional development.[7]

Regardless of how successful the new skill or technique has been and how creative the presentation of the technique is, teachers will still be skeptical. Thomas R. Guskey says that professional development and the adoption of a new technique is actually a series of steps. It is the full sequence that puts the technique into practice.

Demonstrating skills and practices that have changed outcomes is only half of an effective professional development process. In order for those techniques to be permanently incorporated into instructional practice, the students must show progress with the use of these methods, and then teachers' attitudes and expectations change. It is this successful practice that changes beliefs and cements the new techniques into classroom practice.[8]

Creating Organizational Capacity

In order to be effective and change outcomes, staff development must also focus on real students with real problems in real surroundings. "Professional development is the set of knowledge- and skill-building activities that raise the capacity of teachers and administrators to respond to external demands and to engage in the improvement of practice and performance."[9]

The purpose of professional development is not to build individual résumés, but rather to build the skills to improve the capacity of the educational corps. Quality staff development deals with skills and pedagogy that contribute to organizational performance. This is not a résumé enhancement, but a deepening of instructional capacity within the district.

Professional Learning Communities

Frequent meetings of professional learning communities within a protected time frame build organizational capacity. Every teacher has a different personality and often a different approach to classroom teaching. Meeting regularly in the professional learning communities engages the staff in the common purpose.

Professional learning communities (PLCs) within a school may be configured in a way that makes sense for the school. Elementary school PLCs are frequently organized by grade level. Special attention should be given to the inclusion of the teachers who teach multiple grades (physical education, art, music, and sometimes science). The discussion at these meetings can be about issues surrounding an individual student or pedagogy. Since these teachers also teach these students, their perspective is also valuable.

Middle school PLCs can be by grade level, content area, or both. Technique discussion is probably more effective at the content level, and discussion of student progress will work best at the grade level.

At high schools, since the grade levels are less distinct, the professional learning communities are usually formed around content areas (some would call these "departments"). If the district is using the accelerated-learning model, then grade levels will be less distinct at all levels.

The distributed leadership model means that professional development is not only a staff responsibility; it is everyone's job. If you have learned a new way to enhance literacy, you share it. If your class has not understood time and motion in physics, you ask for help. Every teacher has successes and failures. This is not about getting or receiving individual accolades, instead, it is all about coaching and sharing with your PLC to increase the expertise of the entire team.

Finding the Time

Many states require a minimum number of instructional days for students. And while they also specify the amount of seat time required for a unit of instruction (a credit), the number of days and the number of hours can often be manipulated to allow for early-release days. These are days on which the students come to school for the minimum number of hours, so that the day counts as an instructional day, but are sent home early to allow teachers the time for professional development.

Many districts are experimenting with early-release days as a way to schedule protected teacher work days. Since frequent professional development seems to be more effective, consider scheduling an early-release day every week for the purpose.

Agendas for each early release should be prepared in advance by each PLC and submitted to district leadership in case there is a desire to participate. Since administrators and district leadership cannot attend every workshop every day, an electronic attendance form can be used to report which training each staff member received.

It is easy to assume that weekly early release is a chance for teachers to do personal errands that a full teaching load does not allow them to accomplish during the rest of the week. Reinforce the importance of this protected time by allowing excused absences exclusively through the superintendent's office, or in a large district through a specific member of executive staff.

All of your teachers must be given time during their duty days to pursue professional development. This is not an additional responsibility to be added to their already full schedule. Professional development is important, but so is work/life balance. Do not require them to spend less time with their families or friends because you want them to do this.

Resources

In-house expertise is especially useful for professional development. Consider using your in-house drama team to help the teachers present their knowledge in a more understandable and entertaining way. Use of in-house staff is both affirming to the staff and economical.

The content of the professional development should be sourced from outside as well as inside the district. No district is an island of best practices; ideas must be taken from a variety of internal and external sources.

Asking for additional knowledge or skills and sharing the skills and knowledge you have acquired is easier in a culture of collaboration. Contributions to the discussion and to the body of knowledge within your learning community add value.

Professional development is something that many schools and districts do, but few do very well. Do not allow the organization to substitute institutional memory for logical thinking. "The organization's memory embodied in precedents, customs of unknown origin, stories about how things have always been and used to be, and standard operating procedures, becomes used as a substitute for taking wise action."[10]

Leaders

Your organization is a learning organization. Staff, not just students, must continually acquire new knowledge and skills so that the organization can accumulate more knowledge and skills, thereby increasing its instructional capacity.

In his article on evaluating professional development in *Educational Leadership,* Thomas R. Guskey recommends the use of five criteria to evaluate instructional professional development: participants' reaction, participants' learning, organizational support and change, participants' use of new knowledge and skills, and student learning outcomes:

> A lot of good things are done in the name of professional development. But so
> are a lot of rotten things. What educators haven't done is provide evidence to
> document the difference between the two. Evaluation provides the key to
> making that distinction. By including systematic information gathering and
> analysis as a central component of all professional development activities, we
> can enhance the success of professional development efforts everywhere. [11]

Leaders must make that determination of value. Guskey says it doesn't
need to be hard data or proof or improvement, but there should be some
evidence that indicates a positive trend. The evaluation of the professional
development activity should be planned in advance. That way, the collection
of data for evaluation should not be as difficult. If the trend is negative, do
not hesitate. Fix it or drop it. There is nothing more detrimental to teacher
morale than being asked to attend anything less than effective, high quality
training.

As part of the changes she made in her first year as superintendent in San
Diego (California) Unified School District, Cindy Marten decided that professional development for the teachers should be offered at their schools and
not at a location away from their workplace. She then decided that the district's teachers would be better with targeted professional development than
with the consultants that had been contracted to provide the service.

A strong advocate for teachers, Marten has also made teacher accountability part of her message. However, she has garnered support from the
teachers in the field because she obviously trusts them as the most reliable
resource to increase the organization's instructional capacity. She frequently
challenges the district to "dream big, work hard."

Communication

The message connected to professional development is that we don't know
everything, but we intend to continue to learn as much as we can from our
own experts and from other experts in the field. We are radically changing
our methodologies and approach to better prepare our students for life after
graduation, and to do so we will need to retrain ourselves.

Support

Since content knowledge is not the only characteristic of a good teacher, if a
teacher learns something outside of their content area, they also increase the
value of the organization. Targeted professional development (i.e., learning
within a narrow band of assigned content and related skills) is easy to justify
and support. If you are truly a learning organization, shouldn't you also
support the staff continuing their education outside of that narrow spectrum?

Scope

Professional development is district-wide. Both frequency and intensity are important. Every teacher in the district should be given a minimum of two hours of protected and uninterrupted learning every week. This is not teacher-planning time. This time should be used for skills development, data analysis, and meeting with professional learning community colleagues.

Strategy and Reach

The "hire the best and get rid of the rest" attitude is not productive for an educational organization. Professional development is based upon a growth mindset (i.e., giving teachers every opportunity to acquire new skills and knowledge and ultimately to improve their teaching), the same mindset we assume for our students. Remember, performance-based learning is a new system of program delivery, and so every teacher, even the veterans, needs to be retrained.

Best-selling author Barbara Kingsolver has taken a "sabbatical" from writing her novels to write screenplays for two of her most popular works. In speaking about the difficulty of writing a screenplay, even though it was for her own novels, she said, "It's scary to be a beginner again."[12]

If writing in a different format is scary for a writer as accomplished as Kingsolver, think about how difficult it must be for a teacher who may or may not be considered as effective. Creating a safe place to ask for help is crucial for collaboration and productive professional development. Understanding that it is scary is part of that.

Timing

Now is not too soon to improve professional development. The only way to improve outcomes is to change the delivery and the classroom pedagogy. The only way to do that is through high-quality, targeted, and frequent professional development. This touches all three of the key elements of culture enhancement—people, value, and capacity.

Continuum

Professional development must be frequent, continuous, and targeted. It is not an activity that is haphazard or unplanned. A creative and exciting professional development program breathes life into the classroom. Much innovation occurs through connections. By introducing teachers to different skills and methods, you also allow innovation to grow.

Staffing

This is a totally grassroots collaborative effort. No one, meaning everyone, should be in charge of seeking out and delivering high quality programming for professional development. Given the safety of a cooperative professional environment, there should be more development opportunities suggested than there is time to take advantage of.

Assessment and Analysis

The data from the continuous assessments should demonstrate the effectiveness of the professional development program. If the teaching is improving, student progress will improve as well. Keep in mind Jellison's J-Curve. Don't expect immediate improvement. There is always a drop in performance when something new is introduced. It may take a while to increase outcomes.[13]

Logistics

"Encourage your principal, instructional coach, administrator in charge of instruction, whomever makes The Decision about how your school's professional development time and money is spent, to conduct a needs assessment," suggests Rebecca Alber.

Assessment can be fairly simple: asking teachers if they can conceptualize abstract concepts for students, whether they feel knowledgeable about the content they teach, whether they can design a rigorous end-of-course assessment, and whether their teaching style supports diverse learners and learning styles. Get them to share their assessments with their colleagues. Alber writes that this should be the basis of professional development activities—the self-identified needs of the education professionals.[14]

Mistakes

Citing a 2013 National School Boards Association report on professional development, Valerie Strauss in the *Washington Post* says, "Most professional development (PD) is lousy." Supporting teachers during implementation (the steepest learning curve) doesn't happen in the traditional professional development workshop format.[15]

Some Points to Remember about Professional Development

- Expand your view of professional development to include all manner of instruction.
- A lecture format for the presentation of new material is often boring. Separating the audience into smaller groups is not the solution.

- Research indicates that 80 percent of lecture content is lost in two days.
- There are a number of ways to improve presentations if a presentation is needed. Atkinson, Sibbet, and Duarte are but a few of the authors that offer suggestions.
- Knowledge of the methodology is only part of the process to incorporate something new into instructional practice. A teacher's attitude must change. Successful use of the new technique changes attitudes.
- Professional development is for organizational capacity building, not individual resume enhancement.
- Professional learning communities engage staff in a common purpose.
- Use early-release days for professional development.
- Use in-house expertise when possible. In order to increase organizational capacity, the methods presented should come from sources both inside and outside the district.
- Leaders should regularly evaluate the effectiveness of professional development.
- Teachers tend to teach the way they were taught. Professional development is needed to enhance their skills and knowledge.
- These opportunities should be offered to all district staff.
- Part of creating an educational culture is giving instructional staff a safe place to admit they need help.
- Begin improving professional development now.
- The most effective program will be collaborative. Decide if a designated position is really required.
- Conduct a needs assessment to guide professional development.

NOTES

1. Alber, Rebecca. "The Power of Teacher Workshops: Advocating for Better PD at Your School." Edutopia. October 19, 2011. http://www.edutopia.org/blog/better-professional-development-teachers-rebecca-alber (accessed July 10, 2015).

2. "The Curve of Forgetting." AVID online. 2005. http://www.csub.edu/~bruff/The%20Forgetting%20Curve.pdf (accessed November 9, 2015).

3. Atkinson, Cliff. *Beyond Bullet Points*. Redmond, WA: Microsoft Press, 2008.

4. Sibbet, David. *Visual Meetings*. Hoboken, NJ: John Wiley & Sons, 2010.

5. Duarte, Nancy. *Resonate*. Hoboken, NJ: John Wiley & Sons, 2010.

6. Gershenson, Seth. "The Alarming Effect of Racial Mismatch on Teacher Expectations." The Brookings Institution. August 18, 2015. http://www.brookings.edu/blogs/brown-center-chalkboard/posts/2015/08/18-teacher-expectations-gershenson (accessed August 22, 2015).

7. Boes, Cheryl. "Online Teacher Book Clubs: Promoting a Culture of Professional Development." Edutopia. September 3, 2015. http://www.edutopia.org/blog/teacher-book-clubs-promoting-professional-development-cheryl-boes (accessed September 13, 2015).

8. Guskey, T. R. "Does It Make a Difference? Evaluating Professional Development." *Educational Leadership* 59(6), 2002: 45–51.

9. Alber, Rebecca. "The Power of Teacher Workshops."

10. Pfeffer, Jeffrey, and Robert I. Sutton. *The Knowing Doing Gap*. Cambridge, MA: Harvard Business School Publishing, 2000.

11. Guskey, "Evaluating Professional Development."

12. Kingsolver, Barbara, interview by Ann Patchett. "A Conversation with Barbara Kingsolver and Ann Patchett" (at Carolina Mountains Literary Festival) (September 12, 2015).

13. Jellison, Jerald. *Managing the Dynamics of Change*. New York: McGraw-Hill, 2006.

14. Alber, "The Power of Teacher Workshops.

15. Strauss, Valerie. "Why Most Professional Development for Teachers Is Useless." *Washington Post*, March 1, 2014.

Chapter Six

Culture

Excellence is a better teacher than mediocrity. The lessons of the ordinary are everywhere. Truly profound and original insights are to be found only in studying the exemplary.

—Warren Bennis

A quality K–12 educational organization should virtually guarantee that students will be in an academic environment in which they will learn best, they will not be held back because of chronological age, and they will graduate on time from high school.

Intent

If all of your students are graduating and are successful in their careers or college academics, then a change is not necessary. However, if like in most districts, you are continuing to struggle to keep students in school and find that when they get to college, many of them are not successful, then you may want to change your methodology.

The culture of teaching in isolation with traditional methodology has reached the upper limits of its ability to continue to produce better and better results. To advance students and create an environment in which graduation is assured and a student's success after graduation is the rule and not the exception, you must intentionally create a culture of agility and change that responds to the personal needs of every student. That mechanism is performance-based education.

There should be empathy among the staff for each student's struggles, whether they are academic or personal difficulties. The prevailing attitude should be, "Let's find out what's wrong and fix it." The word "blame"

57

cannot be part of the institutional vocabulary. The culture should foster resilience and recovery, regardless of the gravity of the issue.

Failure is only a temporary condition and is literally not an option. There should be a collective expectation that every student can learn and that every student will succeed. If they are not succeeding, the staff can work together to find a better way to change the outcome. Just-in-time multilevel remediation is employed immediately and without hesitation.

There is a professional esprit-de-corps among the educators that comes from working closely with colleagues in weekly professional learning communities. Teachers who begin the year uncomfortable with the cooperative environment will, by the end of the year, be working constructively together to solve problems. It is simply not possible to work in isolation in this environment.

Innovative practice must be the hallmark of the district. Once vetted by the educators, there should never be any hesitation to try a new idea or approach. But innovating is not just about the ideas; it is also about making the adjustments necessary to perfect the ideas. Once again, the cooperative effort of the entire staff is needed to make the ideas as good as possible both before and after they are put into practice.

There has never been a school district listed in the one hundred best places to work published annually in *Fortune*.[1] The analysis and results of this employee survey will provide invaluable information on staff attitudes and organizational culture.

Leaders

Geoff Colvin says, "Culture change starts at the top. As long as those C-level executives think the culture is fine, it will never change."[2]

Innovators always question the status quo. You are developing and commissioning an organization that not only innovates on a regular basis but enjoys it and is purposeful about the results that will follow.

Leading an organization that consistently and without fail will question the status quo can be uncomfortable. Of course, the questioning will be appropriately channeled, and while there won't be hecklers at every staff meeting, leaders should be prepared to explain the logic behind "the way we want to do things around here."

Perhaps you have experience as a parent of when your children asked you "why" so many times that you ultimately said in exasperation, "Because I said so!" Obviously, in this case that's not an option.

As Jerald Jellison suggests, "It is a long and tortuous path instilling the value of change in the organizational culture. Because the trek is repetitive and barrier-ridden, it requires total commitment. You'll say the same thing over and over again. You'll repeatedly need to reward employees when they do the right thing and correct them when they don't."[3]

Asserting that the leader needs a well-rounded team to be successful at change making, John Kotter argues for the creation of a diverse "guiding coalition" that includes position power, expertise, credibility, and leadership with trust and sincerity keeping the team together. Kotter's eight-step process includes:

1. Create a sense of urgency.
2. Build a guiding coalition.
3. Form a strategic vision and initiatives.
4. Enlist a volunteer army.
5. Enable action by removing barriers.
6. Generate short-term wins.
7. Sustain acceleration.
8. Institute change.[4]

Converting a traditional school district to performance-based education involves substantial cultural change, and Kotter's guidance is proven and systematic. Collaborating on classroom instruction, continuously monitoring student progress, creating a safe place for new and different ideas, and taking every opportunity to give students the experience and responsibilities they need to become mature and successful citizens are all part of a culture that supports performance-based learning.

During his cultural-change initiative at a major national insurance organization, one bold CEO told the staff that at the end of two years, they would be asked if they wanted him to stay. He did not take the vote for granted, but he did work very hard to change the culture of his organization, a culture that he believed was counterproductive. When his two years were up, the vote was tallied, and he was overwhelmingly asked to stay. What sort of bold offer could tell your staff that you are committed to this transition?

Communication

There are obviously some issues or information that must be closely held. However, for transparency, the most information must be shared as soon as possible. One of the ways that individuals in an organization exercise power is to withhold information from others. Be sure that everyone affected by any information is informed. Eighty percent of trouble in social interactions comes from a lack of communication.

Cultural change means repetition of the message by rewarding and publicizing the successes. Jellison says, "The leader not only repeats stories of individual accomplishments but he also revels in hearing employees tell him of their successes. Heroes emerge through this process and catchy phrases and slogans too. Listen for the words and phrases you can repeat and use as mottoes and hallmarks of the change."[5]

Refine the message into several concise sentences. One page is too much, and one catchy phrase is too little. This worked for one district: "We put your child into the learning environment in which they can best succeed."

Communication of this intention should hit every parent where they live. As our families have decreased in size, the success of each one of those children has become more and more important. By some descriptions, the baby boomer generation is the first to be unable to give their children a better life than the one they have.[6] This puts tremendous pressure on the parents to do what they can to make their offspring successful. By communicating this as the primary reason for the change in direction, you are synchronizing your message to parents' goals.

But saying is not doing. Most adults today are bombarded with "hype" every day and will see through a message that is not true to reality. Your communication must be a demonstration of what is genuinely going on in the schools. If there is an inconsistency, it will be the program that suffers.

Support

Kotter is matter-of-fact about soliciting support for change. You first identify a highly diverse guiding coalition that cuts across the entire hierarchy in the organization. And then once your strategy is in place, you ask for a volunteer "army."[7]

There is a difference between a community outreach that seeks input and one that seeks support.[8] Demonstrate to the community that your values are in sync with theirs, and ask for their support. This is not to say that some parents and community members won't have great ideas that you can use. Just be clear about what you are soliciting so that everyone is clear about expectations.

The most successful innovators use ideas from all over. This is not strictly an education problem. You must source ideas about how someone in another field created a solution. Tania de Jong from Melbourne, Australia, has introduced her "With One Voice" program to communities all over the world to increase creativity and foster collaboration through singing.[9]

Scope

This culture must be systemic. It is not something nurtured and promoted by a select few early adopters within one or two schools. This will not create a sustainable methodology. Veteran and novice educators alike must understand that they all are learning a different approach and that they are going to perfect it collaboratively. The vision is top down, but the change must be systemic.

Think about the current examples. What if there were different Disney cultures from one theme park to another? How much progress would Google make if each of their departments or offices had a different culture?

This is not optional. There must be a district-wide culture that is innovative, collaborative, professional, and purposeful. Program delivery, assessments, use of technology, professional development, and pedagogy must change.

Strategy and Reach

In a district of three thousand students, the superintendent is able to put his arms around most of the issues that come up. In a district twice that size, some things will exceed the superintendent's grasp (e.g., he would not be able to stop into every teacher's classroom once a week). In an even larger district, it comes down to finding executives and administrators that can create that personal connection with central office for the school staff. These are the individuals who should carry and translate the superintendent's message. That message must be well understood and consistent.

The leadership must be distributed. So, be intentional about targeting delegation throughout the hierarchy of your organization. Each school will need a champion, each high school feeder system will need a creative and committed administrator who has the authority to make the tough decisions. Each of those administrators must have the unwavering support of district leadership.

The conversion to performance-based education means that all of your teachers will have to relearn how to teach.[10] This is why professional development and collaborative improvement are so important. Effective teaching does not occur in isolation but, rather, in full view of and with the cooperation of each educator's professional learning community.

Timing

Recent experiences of those who study change are that many of these steps can occur simultaneously, or at least in a rapid sequence.[11] Most district leaders were not born in the leadership chair and so have a pretty good sense of the capacity and appetite of their district for a cultural change of this magnitude. As a rule of thumb, a year in transition is probably as fast as you want to move, and three years is probably as long as you want to take. The important issue in terms of timing is to not lose momentum.

Continuum

Despite your best efforts, district leadership will turn over an average of every 3.6 years. The American Association of School Administrators reported in their 2010 survey that 51 percent of superintendents that responded indicated they planned on leaving the superintendency by 2015.[12] Given this situation, designating leadership succession will be necessary for continued program success. Otherwise performance-based education and all its benefits will be a short-lived 3.6-year experiment.

Staffing

Administrators should staff for cultural fit and attitude, not an impressive résumé or similar experience. While educational experience tends to be more important in a traditional program-delivery environment, it is of less relevance than having a strong team player, since you are not continuing a traditional educational culture.

Jellison says there are three groups of people that emerge from a change effort:

1. Ready to wear. These are the enthusiastic adopters.
2. Wait and see. Halfhearted compliance.
3. Resisters. These are the opponents.

He cautions us to not invert our efforts, spending 80 percent of our time trying to convince the 20 percent of resisters that the change is logical. In fact, logic may not have anything to do with why these people are resisting.[13]

Do not neglect the importance of getting staff on board for cultural change. New staff properly taken on board can be strong allies in the transition. After all, the new culture is one of the reasons they have decided to work for you!

Assessment and Analysis

The only way to assess culture change is through observation and anonymous survey results. The key is to develop and pose the questions in a variety of ways in order to develop trends from the responses. There are software programs that can help.[14]

Most state education departments are now doing school-climate surveys. These will give you some basic information and at least provide a double check against your own, more detailed data.

Don't neglect informal conversation at the lunch table. It is an important source of information. Executives should attend lunch with the staff as frequently as possible. This provides an opportunity to get staff feedback, but also an opportunity to gauge the depth and breadth of the transition (one or two of the staff rolling their eyes probably means the message needs to be tweaked).

Logistics

There are two ways of viewing intelligence and learning. The first is a *fixed mindset*. Those with a fixed mindset believe their intelligence is a fixed asset. To students with this mindset, risk is something to avoid because they may perform poorly or it may cause them to demonstrate their deficiencies. "Finally, students with a fixed mindset do not handle setbacks well. Because they believe that setbacks call their intelligence into question, they become defensive or discouraged when they don't succeed right away."[15] Tracking and deficit thinking both come from a belief in fixed intelligence.

The other view of intelligence is a *growth mindset*. These students believe that their hard work allows them to learn and grow. Their intelligence is not a fixed asset, but something that can be nurtured and will grow with meaningful work. A growth-mindset culture in the classroom is supported and reinforced by praising a student's process and persistence and not their ability.

The good news is that these mindsets are not cast in stone. A growth mindset can be developed. Teachers can create a culture of growth by introducing meaningful and challenging work and then describing that work as informative. This work could include phrases that indicate that barriers are not failures, but learning opportunities.[16] Part of the cultural change is to develop a growth-mindset culture. This alone will raise expectations.

Celebrate the things that didn't work as well as those that did. Why? It is the only way to create a safe space for staff to innovate.

Mistakes

Inconsistency in word or action is the biggest mistake you can make in cultural change. It signals that the change is not authentic, and therefore not long lasting. The "ready-to-wear" folks will feel betrayed, the "wait-and see" folks will feel vindicated, and the "resisters" will begin celebrating.

Although cultural change is a serious business with a serious purpose, fun must be part of the transition as well. Purposeful work is a joy. And that joy should be expressed formally and informally, but frequently. It can be playful or serious fun. One district executive whose presentation to a board meeting ran twice as long as planned was given a sundial as an "award."

Some Points to Remember about Culture

- Regular work in professional learning communities promotes collaboration and esprit-de-corps among educators. Isolation is not an option.

- Innovative practices should be encouraged and celebrated.
- Culture starts at the top. If your executives think everything is fine, it will never change.
- Leading an organization that continuously innovates is sometimes intimidating because the status quo is always being questioned.
- Create a diverse coalition to guide the work. The culture must be systemic and pervasive throughout the district.
- Intentionally create a culture of agility and change that responds to the personal needs of every student. Refine and repeat the message. Be consistent.
- Informally review the culture frequently.
- Don't forget to have fun.

NOTES

1. "Learn What It Takes." Great Places to Work. 2015. http://www.greatplacetowork.com/best-companies/100-best-companies-to-work-for (accessed July 22, 2015).

2. Colvin, Geoff. *Talent Is Overrated*. New York: Penguin Group, 2008.

3. Jellison, Jerald. *Managing the Dynamics of Change*. New York: McGraw-Hill, 2006.

4. Kotter, John P. *Leading Change*. Cambridge, MA: Harvard Business School Press, 1996.

5. Jellison, *Managing the Dynamics of Change*.

6. Lowrey, Annie. "Younger Generations Lag Parents in Wealth-Building." *New York Times*, March 14, 2013: B1.

7. Kotter, *Leading Change*.

8. Bleiker, Hans, Annamarie Bleiker, and Jennifer Bleiker. *Citizen Participation Handbook*. Monterey: Institute for Participatory Management and Planning, 2012.

9. de Jong, Tania. "With One Voice." 2015. http://www.creativityaustralia.org.au/ (accessed November 30, 2015).

10. Elmore, Richard F. *School Reform from the Inside Out*. Cambridge, MA: Harvard University Press, 2004.

11. Kotter, John P. *Accelerate*. Boston: Harvard Business School Publishing, 2014.

12. Kowalski, Theodore J., Robert S. McCord, George J. Peterson, I. Phillip Young, and Noelle M. Ellerson. "The American School Superintendent: 2010 Decennial Study." Alexandria, VA: American Association of School Administrators, 2010.

13. Jellison, *Managing the Dynamics of Change*.

14. PeopleSpark. 2015. http://peoplespark.com/ (accessed November 29, 2015).

15. Dweck, Carol S. "Even Geniuses Work Hard." *Educational Leadership* 66(1), 2010: 16–20.

16. Ibid.

Chapter Seven

Collaboration

If you want to build a ship, don't drum up people together to collect wood and don't assign them tasks and work, but rather teach them to long for the endless immensity of the sea.

—Antione de Saint-Exupéry

Collaboration begins with an attitude adjustment: this is not my problem or your problem, but *our* problem, and we will work to solve it together. The current concept of teaching, that it is a profession that is practiced in isolation and is either done well or poorly, is detrimental and counterproductive to education.

Intent

Student success is the obvious overriding purpose. Collaboration among the staff and students is simply part of doing business more effectively. Certified staff should model collaboration by working together to improve everyone's classroom practice and increasing the probability of student success.

Practice

For any educational institution to judge some teachers as good while others are not, is certainly contrary to what they say they believe about their students. "Hire and retain the best," a slogan that has been pervasive in the push to improve public education, assumes that effectiveness is an innate quality that some teachers have and some don't. Or worse, that by shining the spotlight of accountability on every teacher, those who are intentionally not meeting standards will somehow miraculously improve.

Richard Elmore argues that since all teachers learn and practice virtually the same techniques, that all yield less than optimum results, every teacher needs to be taught a better set of different skills.[1]

He maintains that there is little difference in the instructional quality between the successful schools and the failing schools. The difference is in socioeconomic backgrounds of the students and not in the proficiency of the teachers. The national correlation between family income and academic outcomes certainly seems to bear that out.

Every student's struggle is a team challenge. Each teacher should work within their professional learning community to explore new techniques, perfecting those that seem to hold promise for improving student outcomes, and identifying specific strategies for those students who are struggling to keep up.

Students, teachers, administrators, and executive staff must collaborate to improve. They should focus on how the current methods are working for real students in real classrooms and the analysis of continuous assessment data from those students. The search should be both outward and inward. What are *we* doing? How can we do better? What are *others* doing? How can we incorporate it into our practice?

Carrie Leana, in her article in the *Stanford Social Innovation Review*, discusses building social capital through collaboration as the Missing Link in School Reform. She says, "after decades of failed programs aimed at improving student achievement through teacher human capital and principal leadership, such investments in social capital are cheap by comparison and offer far more promise of measurable gains for students."[2]

Celebrate successful collaboration. Teacher teams should be asked to present their methodology to their colleagues during protected professional development. Teachers who model successful collaboration should be eligible to receive formal recognition for their contributions to student success. An attitude of empathy should exemplify the staff and be demonstrated over and over in their actions.

Leana finds that "in many schools, such social capital is assumed to be an unaffordable luxury or, worse, a sign of teacher weakness or inefficiency. Yet our research suggests that talking to peers about the complex task of instructing students is an integral part of every teacher's job and results in rising student achievement."[3] Mentorships, professional learning communities, and team teaching are just some of the ways social capital is built.

Leadership

Successful leaders know that effective collaborators are team players. They are neither ego driven nor ambitious career climbers. These professionals are happy to work with their colleagues to focus on the job at hand and the long-term struggle of helping each and every student become successful. They handle the urgent without losing sight of the important.

In their article in *Educational Leadership*, researchers Shirley M. Hord and Stephanie A. Hirsh suggest principals support strong learning communities by:

- Confirming teachers' ability to succeed together, but making it clear that to do so they will need to pool their expertise;
- Expecting teachers to keep their knowledge fresh and current through collaborative study;
- Guiding communities toward self-direction by distributing leadership;
- Making data on student performance accessible and easy to understand;
- Helping teachers develop skills in talking and making decisions together;
- Sharing the research on professional learning communities—teachers reap benefits like shared responsibility for student success, increased understanding of teachers' roles in helping students achieve, feedback and assistance from peers, and professional renewal; and
- Giving teachers guided practice in conducting appropriate conversations, making decisions, and managing conflict will help strengthen trust, so will keeping the focus on building student and teacher learning. [4]

Building social capital through a culture of collaboration is a process of continuous improvement. It will not happen because you order it to happen; it will happen over time as teachers and administrators realize working together toward student success is far more rewarding and actually more effective than an individual effort.

Recognition and rewards should be set aside primarily for teams and not as an "if/then" protocol. When individuals are recognized, it should be because they are team players.

Communication

The messaging around collaboration is very straightforward. "It is not a sign of weakness to ask for help. It is better to collaborate with colleagues to solve a problem than to struggle with it in isolation. Team players succeed and should be recognized and rewarded." Simple.

The executive team should lead by example. Guests should be invited to executive staff meetings to demonstrate how district leadership collaborates effectively. Invite a few teachers to be guests into each executive staff meeting. Model vulnerability within executive staff by asking for and offering help to one another.

During the meeting, the superintendent should model vulnerability (ask for help) at least once at each meeting. This is not to ask for coffee or for volunteers, but to be genuine about asking for assistance or advice.

Clearly, collaboration also involves a sea change in how you view teaching. If effective teaching is seen as individual expertise and something that you either have or you don't, then collaboration on the scale discussed has no reason to occur. Just as teachers must have a growth mindset in regard to their students, so too they must understand that good teaching is also learned, and not part of someone's DNA.

Support

Teams are not successful without providing support to the members that need it. Support comes in all shapes and sizes:

- Support is taking bus duty for a colleague who is still learning the grade book software.
- Support is temporarily team teaching with a staff member who is worried about a sick child at home and may need to leave in the middle of the day.
- Support is providing snacks for your PLC meeting, knowing you will be analyzing new student data today.
- Support is still largely composed of individual effort, but it is focused on building social capital and not self-improvement.

A collaborative culture is a long-term movement. All of the issues that foster teacher competition and impede collaboration are typically out of district control and will still exist—low pay, high stakes testing, teacher effectiveness ratings, and the assignment of letter grades to schools.

A culture of collaboration can still be nurtured and encouraged within the district, but it is not just mentioning it once at the start of the school year that will create the culture. Day after day, year after year it needs to be modeled, celebrated, discussed, and reinforced. Creating and supporting professional learning communities within the district is one way to do this.

Scope

Building social capital is a district-wide effort. The change from a traditional educational culture (in which individual capital is built) to one in which social capital is built cannot occur in groups of early adopters or just as a product of a compliance mindset. For the team players, this is easy. For those who prefer to teach in isolation, it is more difficult. But collaboration must be a complete cultural change within the district, not simply something that some individuals do.

Strategy and Reach

Dr. Brené Brown, in her books and TED talks, says that admitting vulnerability can create that safe place where someone can say they need help. [5] Professional networking and collaboration are healthy activities for educators. Isolating educators, either physically in their classrooms or theoretically by not endorsing a growth mindset, is detrimental to their practice.

Like innovation, which requires both inward and outward vision, without the input and crosstalk from colleagues, instruction tends to become routine, uninspired, and quickly dated. Emphasizing collaboration to improve social capital keeps instructional practice fresh and current.

Elmore blames the loosely coupled structure of most educational organizations (originally put in place to protect instructional practice from the vagaries of state and local politics) for the inability of reform efforts to change what happens in the classroom. If the goal is a significant improvement of academic outcomes and not just minimal improvement in "trends," then classroom pedagogy must change. [6]

The reach in this case must be deep and long. Performance-based learning requires a thorough reexamination of instructional practice and a major effort in professional development eliminating the ineffective and celebrating the practices that show potential. Collaboration makes changing instructional delivery possible.

Timing

This is one of the few aspects of the book where just talking about it might actually be beneficial. Begin the discussions now. Like every successful reform effort, the discussion should begin with questions. They can be as innocent as, "How might we collaborate with others to keep our students in school?" or as direct as "How might we change our educational methodology to something more collaborative in order to improve our outcomes and have zero dropouts? What have others done?"

This is stimulating sustenance for educators. Once you begin the questions, it is not likely that the discussions will stop. Continue prodding the dialogue. Keep a close eye on the organizational appetite and fervor. Once it reaches urgency, start talking about implementation. Development and support (time within the duty day) of effective professional learning communities (PLCs) is a quick win for collaboration.

Continuum

Just like a wood fire in the fire pit on a chilly winter evening, the fire of collaborative effort must be carefully and frequently tended. The fuel can't be too big, or too wet, or too incendiary. However, it must be periodically stoked or stirred.

Professional collaboration is a thoughtful process. For those organizations with access to data, carefully analyzing new student data perpetuates the work. You will never really reach a point where collaboration is no longer necessary. The good news is that once it becomes part of the educational environment, it will be hard to eradicate.

Staffing

Much of the "on-boarding" effort in many districts focuses on the details of employment with very little time spent on acculturation. New staff, although they may be team players, will nevertheless believe that asking for help will be viewed as a sign of weakness.

Use this opportunity of bringing on board new staff to make them familiar with your culture. Tell them to ask for help and that the veteran staff will not think less of them for asking. Use the beginning of the school year each year to remind staff of the same expectations.

Attention should also be paid to the staff that is hired during the school year. In a small district, this may be just a handful of people. In a large district, it can be a substantial contingent. On-boarding is just as important for these individuals as for those who were hired before the school year began.

There are other ways to include staff. For several years, Charlotte-Mecklenburg Schools selected about ten high-potential first- and second-year Teach for America teachers to intern with a member of the executive staff during the summer. This small experiment helped to humanize the daunting bureaucracy of the big district. Could you do something similar in your district?

Assessment and Analysis

Use collaborative time to analyze student data. Assessment is a continuous process, so easy-to-analyze timely data on student progress is essential.

Logistics

Consider instituting regular early-release days. This will be protected professional development time for certified staff. It will give each professional learning community a chance to meet and collaborate, to improve student progress, and address concerns. Set aside this time for only one purpose and reinforce its importance by making the superintendent the only one that can excuse an absence. Prepare topics and agendas in advance, and send to the central office in case a member of executive staff wants to attend.

Allow teachers and students the use of their cell phones. How does this help with collaboration? When a principal wants his or her staff to get timely information, they will send an e-mail or a text message. If there is something staff should know, they will know it immediately.

Many school districts are experimenting with different forms of early-release schedules to promote professional development. Don't use the time just to lecture to the assembled staff, use most of the professional development time for collaboration in small professional learning communities. This allows for individual participation and building collaborative social capital.

Celebrate collaboration by recognizing group contributions and rewarding collaborative efforts. Encourage collaboration by making space available in schools for small informal gatherings. Give teachers a chance to socialize within the daily schedule. Above all, realize that teacher dialogue in the hallway is something to be encouraged as it promotes the social network that ultimately supports the students.

Many teachers find it hard to find affordable housing. Consider subsidizing or seeking corporate subsidies for multiunit housing for teachers. This will not only relieve some of the stress of day-to-day expenses but will also increase collaboration and support among your most vulnerable staff.

Mistakes

It is just as hard to admit a mistake as it is to ask for help. Both make us feel vulnerable and inadequate. Some of that has to do with the way the help is ultimately offered. An attitude of superiority in providing any help that is requested is detrimental to collaboration. Help should be offered without judgement. No one has all of the answers in this ever-changing educational and technical landscape. Eventually, everyone has to ask for help.

Some Points to Remember about Collaboration

- Collaboration, not just cooperation, is an essential component of creating a version of performance-based education. Research indicates that building social capital is far more effective than human capital for improving results. [7]
- Successful collaborators are neither ego driven nor ambitious career climbers, but effective team players.
- Creating professional learning communities and giving them the chance to meet frequently is an opportunity to enhance collaboration. Like innovation, which requires both inward and outward vision, without the input and crosstalk from colleagues, instruction tends to become routine, uninspired, and quickly dated.
- It is not a sign of weakness or lack of proficiency to admit you need help.

- Use on-boarding activities for acculturation.
- Give teachers access to easy-to-analyze student data.
- Increase protected professional development time.
- To improve communication, permit cell phones to be used within the schools.
- Create intentional education communities by making affordable group housing available to beginning teachers.
- Vulnerability should be modeled by veteran educators and administrators, and help should be offered without an attitude of superiority in order to foster a safe place to ask for help.

NOTES

1. Elmore, Richard F. *School Reform from the Inside Out*. Cambridge, MA: Harvard University Press, 2004.

2. Leana, Carrie R. "The Missing Link in School Reform." *The Stanford Social Innovation Review* 9(4), 2011.

3. Ibid.

4. Hord, Shirley M., and Stephanie A. Hirsh. "The Principal's Role in Supporting Learning Communities." *Educational Leadership* 66(5), 2009: 22–23.

5. Brown, Dr. Brené. *Daring Greatly: How the Courage to Be Vulnerable Transforms the Way We Live, Love, Parent, and Lead*. New York: Gotham Books, 2012.

6. Elmore, *School Reform from the Inside Out*.

7. Leana, "The Missing Link in School Reform."

Chapter Eight

Continuous Validation

Treat a man as he is and he will remain as he is; treat a man as he can and should be and he will become as he can and should be.

—Goethe

What is continuous validation and why is it important? Continuous validation is the frequent affirmation from administrators and teachers that one's work is of consequence. Praise for the process (and not the person) is a source of personal and professional motivation. It can simply be a sign of professional courtesy and respect.

Purpose

Recognition of a job well done or of an accomplishment that is perfectly aligned to the organization's goals reinforces employee commitment and engagement. Because continuous validation is an excellent motivator, in successful districts there is an enthusiasm for the work to be done and excitement about making every student successful. What is the atmosphere in your district?

Within the spectrum of continuous validation is respect. Almost every organization's values statement refers to respect. Some say that staff should respect one another regardless of their position in the company. Others talk about respect in communication and in working relationships. But as Michael Burchell and Jennifer Robin explain in their book, *The Great Workplace*, it's not about rules or enforcement, but about attitude.

Employees in great places to work say things like:

- "The owners are very involved—more so than in any other company I have worked for. They work very hard to show appreciation to the employees and give back to the employees and the community"; or
- "I feel that the company truly cares about their employees and recognizes their efforts."

How would you feel if one of your teachers or students said, "I'm given resources even before I know I need them. They set us up to be successful."[1]

If the ability to recognize good work is distributed throughout the organization, then recognition and reward can be more timely and meaningful. Burchell and Robin believe that making recognition and reward personal to the employee can make it even more meaningful. Personalized and on-the-spot awards can score quick wins with employees by building trust.[2]

Gallup research actually confirms that staff receiving recognition and praise within the last seven days demonstrate increased productivity and are more engaged at work.[3]

For this reason alone, continuous validation makes sense. Teaching and learning is a daily challenge. Results may not be immediate, and so the work can be very frustrating. Motivated students and faculty exhibit resilience when their work is frequently recognized.

Praise feels good. Many administrators and teachers use recognition effectively to motivate their staff and students. But there are times when the words of even the most eloquent of motivators fail to yield a good result. Here are a few recommendations:

- Recognize good efforts and effective strategies and praise them.
- Be specific about the praised behaviors.
- Reinforce behavior with feedback.
- Connect the outcomes of an assignment to efforts.
- Be explicit about the strategies that have been used: What worked? What didn't?
- Demonstrate value by asking for an explanation of the work.
- Do not praise trivial accomplishments or weak effort because it is not productive.
- Inflated praise is not helpful, particularly for individuals with low self-esteem.
- Treat each challenge as an opportunity for learning—those with learning difficulties should not be made to feel ashamed.
- Do praise the work someone has done, not their intelligence (e.g., "your argument is very clear" or "your homework is very accurate," but never "you are so smart").
- Don't comfort someone following a failure by telling them that not everyone can be good at everything.[4]

Make continuous validation routine, but spontaneous. Recognize good work. The team will improve as a result.

Leadership

Everyone wants their team to be an A team. There are simply not enough A players to go around. Sometimes even a team of A players ends up performing like a B team. Sometimes a B team plays like an A team. What makes the difference?

In his article in *Harvard Business Review,* Tomas Chamorro-Premuzic says, "Good leaders can turn B players into an A team, by following the right strategy, gathering precise performance data, giving accurate feedback, and building and maintaining high morale."[5]

Continuous validation creates and maintains that high morale for staff and students. Everyone seeks validation for the work they do, whether it is a teacher spending additional time with a student who is struggling or a student working harder to master the principles of physics.

Although all leadership behavior may be subject to some interpretation, Dr. Richard W. Scholl developed a list of "affirming behaviors" that he believes are generally interpreted to be validating:

- Sharing important information with you; indicating trusting behavior is one of the most validating types of behavior;
- Asking for advice;
- Following one's advice;
- Indicating that somebody is glad to see you through facial expressions or body language;
- Including you in events and activities;
- Giving positive feedback and recognition of your skills and worth;
- Choosing to spend time with you when there are other motivating options—when you perceive that an individual incurs a cost in choosing between you and another activity, it increases the affirming nature of the choice;
- Showing concern for your well-being;
- Taking time to listen to your problems and showing empathy;
- Showing deference, respect, and acknowledgment of status;
- Recognizing significant achievements; and
- Remembering important things about you.[6]

You will notice that these are not grand or costly gestures, but everyday acts of kindness and respect. Nonetheless, this type of gesture forms the basis of a professional working relationship with the educators in your district and engenders a student's engagement with their school.

Find a method for remembering names. In a large district the fact that the superintendent or assistant superintendent can remember your name is also a point of personal validation.

Communication

Recognition and validation must be specific and timely. It doesn't help to recognize the state champion football team a full year after they won. It is less effective to give kudos to a teacher for accomplishing National Board Certification six months after they have earned it. Thanking everyone for their hard work on a project is an attitude of gratitude and a start, but thanking each individual and identifying specifically what they did to accomplish the work two days ago is validation.

Support

A discussion of a performance evaluation is probably not something you would expect to be included in a section under support, but evaluations are one way to support continuous validation. Marc Effron and Miriam Ort in their book, *One Page Talent Management,* describe a timely and uncomplicated method of talent management. "We believe the solution lies in radically simplifying and adding value to talent management practices to ensure their implementation and release their scientifically proven power."[7]

Can an evaluation really be a means of validation? Of course. The protocol that Effron and Ort have designed identifies the positives and deficiencies and then sorts for the handful of deficiencies that are most egregious and actionable.

Do this on a monthly basis. (It's only one page!) Discuss the positives first. Then discuss one actionable issue to work on. This is not as scientific as the methodology in the book, but the purpose is different. It is another way to provide continuous validation. It also makes the other more traditional evaluations less traumatic.

Scope

Continuous validation should be district-wide and personal. "I really appreciate all the hard work that the teachers are doing," is effective, but clearly less powerful than, "Have you seen all the cool stuff that Ms. Green is doing in sixth grade math?"

But like everything else discussed here, the comment must be authentic. If Ms. Green is doing what everyone else is doing in sixth grade math, the results of the comment will be disastrous. "Why did Ms. Green get special attention? What's going on?"

Strategy and Reach

The strategy is to identify all the good work that is going on in the district, acknowledge it, and (if possible) reward it. Again, the reward system does not need to be extravagant or costly, but it must be specific, timely, and personal. This lubricates the wheels of progress toward the district's goals. If you do something very difficult at great personal cost and it is not recognized, how likely are you to repeat the effort?

This is not strictly a top-down effort. Recognition can be 360 degrees. Each staff member should be able to recognize good work done by a direct report, a coworker, or a leader. Google employees are empowered to recognize a peer for extraordinary work. They can electronically recognize a coworker with a $150 "peer bonus."[8]

Timing

Timely recognition of accomplishment is essential to making this work. A week is far better than two weeks beyond the event. An annual event is only powerful if it is connected to a more continuous flow of recognition. If school newspapers are composed and distributed digitally, they can be a timely source of information as well as acknowledgment.

The Duke University basketball team was invited to the White House in September 2015 and recognized for their March 2015 championship. While still meaningful, it wasn't news.

Continuum

This is not event specific. An annual awards banquet is not a system of continuous validation. District leadership should model personal recognition of staff and students on a regular basis. In the absence of specific details, a blanket statement of appreciation is certainly acceptable, but *only* when you don't have detailed information.

When talking to staff members, if you have a habit of thanking them for the work they do, or of telling them how much you appreciate what they do, you must change the way you express that. Do not use the same terminology each time. Even though the sentiment might be heartfelt, saying the same words to each individual does not convey it authentically.

Mix it up: Thank you for what you do. I really appreciate your hard work on this. You really nailed this one, thanks. Great job. Nice work today. You always know just what to do. It is obvious how much you enjoy what you do. Thanks for being so well prepared today. We make a good team, I really appreciate your help.

Staffing

Empathetic individuals are best at this. They seem to have a sense of just what to say and how to say it. Team players and coaches can do this, too. Command-and-control people will probably need some help on this aspect of leadership. This is a skill that a mentor can help you improve.

Schedule a second orientation course during which employees who have been with the organization about two months can discuss their experiences to date. Include a no-holds-barred question-and-answer session. This will help new staff realize that what they are experiencing is similar to others' experiences, and listening for information will give the organization a better understanding of the issues new hires face.

Assessment and Analysis

Formal and informal climate surveys are the best sources of information for this aspect of performance-based education. This is a data dashboard item that district personnel see daily. Frequency should obviously be much more often than once a year.

Logistics

To accomplish continuous validation, particularly in a larger school system, a communication pipeline must be put into place to discover what the staff and students have done. It should be easy to upload text and/or photos or to get comments from school leaders. This pipeline is for receiving information, not publishing it. Once received, the information can be distributed to the appropriate school administrators and staff members.

How the information is processed depends upon each individual. Some may prefer to informally recognize the accomplishment; others may want to do a more formal recognition. Principals may want to find and recognize a student during class change. Clearly the recognition should fit the accomplishment (and these are not necessarily all academic accomplishments).

Mistakes

Even continuous validation has its pitfalls. It is a mistake for everyone to receive a "trophy" just for showing up. Praising all work, regardless of quality, devalues good work. Decide whether you will recognize the effort, the outcomes, or both.

In each case, use the opportunity to reward and reinforce those activities that are aligned with the district's goals. If an employee has worked hard but failed, how should their work be validated? If an employee has succeeded in a task because of a serendipitous twist of fate, how should they be praised? Should their "good fortune" or "improvement" be acknowledged or ignored?

Some Points to Remember about Continuous Validation

- Continuous validation is the frequent affirmation from administrators and teachers that one's work is of consequence. Recognition of good work is a way of showing respect for the work of teachers and students and motivating them to continue to do good work.
- Praise process, not people. Recognize effort, not abilities.
- Be specific and timely (within a week of the accomplishment if possible).
- Continuous validation is not event specific, but serendipitous.
- Use frequent one-page evaluations to reinforce and encourage good work.
- Do not use the same language to praise every time. It lacks authenticity. Empathetic individuals are best at this.
- Schedule a second orientation for new employees about two months into their employment. The discussion will make them realize that what they are experiencing is not atypical. Do not neglect to onboard midyear hires.
- Keep the results of climate surveys on a dashboard for district personnel as a reminder.
- Keep the pipelines of information open in order to identify good work.

NOTES

1. Burchell, Michael, and Jennifer Robin. *The Great Workplace*. San Francisco: Jossey-Bass, 2011.

2. Ibid.

3. Rath, Tom, and Barry Conchie. *Strengths Based Leadership*. New York: Gallup Press, 2008.

4. Dwyer, Carol, Carol Dweck, and Heather Carlson-Jaquez. "Using Praise to Enhance Student Resilience and Learning Outcomes." American Psychological Association. n.d. http://www.apa.org/education/k12/using-praise.aspx (accessed October 30, 2015).

5. Chamorro-Premuzic, Tomas. "How to Manage a Team of B Players." *Harvard Business Review*, July 13, 2015. https://hbr.org/2015/07/how-to-manage-a-team-of-b-players.

6. Scholl, Richard W. "Motivation: Affirming Behavior." the University of Rhode Island Web Notes. 2004. http://www.uri.edu/research/lrc/scholl/webnotes/Motivation_Affirming.htm (accessed July 9, 2015).

7. Effron, Marc, and Miriam Ort. *O ne Page Talent Management*. Cambridge, MA: Harvard Business School Publishing, 2010.

8. Robin Young. "Technologies and Philosophies Changing the Workplace." *Here and Now*. September 2, 2015. https://hereandnow.wbur.org/2015/09/02/technology-changing-the-workplace (accessed September 3, 2015).

Chapter Nine

Assessment and Data

Without data you're just another person with an opinion.

— W. Edwards Deming

Continuous assessments are diagnostic. Their purpose is to measure student progress and to make adjustments to instruction. "Think of assessment, then, as information for improving. This idea takes a while to get used to if you teach, test, and move on. The research could not be clearer, though: Increasing formative assessment is the key to improvement on tests of all kinds, including traditional ones."[1]

Intent

Continuous assessment develops real-time data about how much content a student has learned and can apply. By knowing this, the student and the teacher can collaborate to adjust instruction, either making up the deficit or accelerating the pace. Ultimately, knowing where you are allows you to map your journey to where you want to be.

Practice

There are two types of tests—formative and summative. Formative assessments are those that teachers prepare and use to measure progress toward an academic objective. The results of formative testing are a learning tool for the student and information for the teacher about the effectiveness of the lesson. For that reason, the results are usually not made public, although they are shared with the student and their family.

Formative tests are called "criterion-referenced" tests because they are measuring student performance against a predetermined set of criteria. Although some formative assessments are purchased by a district and given to more than one class (Measures of Academic Progress is one source), they are more often created by a teacher and used only in his or her classroom. When formatives are used effectively, they can be leading indicators of future outcomes on high-stakes tests.

Summative assessments are used to measure a student's accumulated knowledge of a specific content and are most often used as end-of-grade or end-of-course tests. Summatives can be criterion-referenced tests, but are usually norm-referenced tests used to compare the test taker or their educational entity (school, district, state, etc.) to another. Because they are comprehensive in nature and used for comparisons, summatives are often called "high-stakes" tests. These results are made public and used as measures of quality of the education being provided.

The current resistance to the proliferation of high-stakes testing is about summatives that are a result of the Common Core curriculum. Parents, students, and many teachers and administrators feel that far too much time is being spent on preparing for and taking these norm-referenced tests. And to add insult to injury, some legislators are using these results to rate the effectiveness of schools and assigning letter grades to the schools based in large part upon these tests.

But no matter what method of program delivery is used, formative assessments occur several times during every class. They may not be called that, but teachers are constantly measuring their students' knowledge and skills against an agreed upon criteria. The criteria could be a pacing guide written by the state education department or something created by the teacher or the district. There is almost always a measurement of progress against a standard.

In a blog post in the *New York Times*, Annie Murphy Paul discusses five strategies that she believes will not only help students do well on tests but actually help them use the tests as a learning tool:

> Used correctly, tests can help students achieve three crucial aims: supporting student recall (tests force students to pull information from their own heads, enhancing retention); enhancing their awareness of their own mental processes (in the process of being tested and getting feedback, students fine-tune their sense of what they know and don't know); and nurturing the noncognitive skills students develop from facing challenges (tests represent a kind of controlled adversity, an ideal arena for honing skills like resilience and perseverance).

Paul says self-testing aids retrieval. And while retrieval may be the most basic of skills, it does engender learning, helps with retention of knowledge, and also improves academic performance. Self-testing has been shown to be more effective than simply rereading as a method of study.

She also recommends interval studying, rather than cramming. Studying in this way actually increases retention, particularly if the student is self-testing as a means of study. What happens is that some facts are lost in the interval when studying does not occur, and the work of relearning those facts strengthens the knowledge.

A technique called "interleaving"—that is, shuffling all variations of content practice problems—helps students diagnose the type of problem and what they are being asked to accomplish.

Paul also suggests the use of what is called an "exam wrapper" when teachers return a corrected test to a student. "The instructions lead students through the process of reflecting on how well they prepared for the test, how well they performed and what they will do differently next time." The corrected test and wrapper then become another tool to study for an upcoming test.

The final recommendation regards calming test anxiety by using the ten minutes prior to a test as an expressive writing exercise about whatever is on students' minds. Research indicates this technique reduces anxiety and increases performance.[2]

Since performance-based education requires students to demonstrate mastery of content, teachers concentrate on affirmative testing that avoids multiple-choice or true/false answers. Questions in class and in the exercises encourage the application of acquired knowledge to new problems and higher order thinking, not memorization.

There are many software applications available to assist teachers in the preparation and evaluation of tests and quizzes. One application by Google called Google Forms provides immediate feedback to both the teacher and student. The Google script Flubaroo grades the assessments that have been submitted and also organizes students' responses into a spreadsheet.

It is not sufficient for the teacher alone to possess all of the data from testing. It is important that the data be shared with the students and given to the students' families so that everyone knows what is expected and what progress has been made. But before they can share, teachers and administrators must understand and know how to analyze the data.

This is where professional development and technical support apply. Information about students and their performance is of no use if the teachers do not use it or do not understand how to interpret it. Targeted professional development is necessary to give the educators a basic knowledge of the field.

The student-progress data should be easily accessed, timely, and well organized so that teachers can easily interpret and analyze the results. Technical advisors can be helpful in assisting the teachers with report formats.

Analysis of data can occur every week at every level through various professional learning communities. School principals can report weekly to central office administrators about future plans for professional development and past results of data analysis across grade-level or content-level professional learning communities.

Leaders

Dr. Kelvin Adams is in his ninth year as superintendent of the St. Louis (Missouri) Public Schools. He credits a data-driven approach to getting that school district on the road to full accreditation with the state. "One of the greatest successes in the last few years is having a different mindset about looking at data," he says, "It's not always about what you feel makes for better education, it's about what the data says."[3]

In their article in *Phi Delta Kappan,* Rick Stiggins and Dan Duke write, "Instructional leadership also requires an understanding of the role of sound assessment in efforts to improve teaching and learning." Their conclusion is that classroom assessments must be applied almost continuously in order to gauge student progress toward a standard. The assessment array must provide decision makers with different kinds of information at different times and in different forms to substantiate student progress toward learning.[4]

Stephen Chappius and his associates outlined the following ten assessment competencies in *Assessment for Learning: An Action Guide for School Leaders*. According to them, a school leader should be able to do the following:

- Understand how assessments are used in support of learning and work with staff to integrate them into classroom instruction.
- Understand the need for clear academic achievement targets and their relationship to the development of accurate assessments.
- Know and evaluate the teacher's classroom assessment competencies and help them learn to assess accurately and use the results productively.
- Plan, present, or secure professional development activities that contribute to the use of appropriate assessment practices.
- Analyze student assessment information accurately, use the information to improve curriculum and instruction, and assist teachers to do the same.
- Develop and implement sound assessment and assessment-related policies.
- Create the conditions necessary for the appropriate use and reporting of student achievement information, and communicate effectively with all members of the school community about student assessment results and their relationship to improving curriculum and instruction.
- Understand the standards of quality for student assessments and how to verify their use in their school and district assessments.
- Understand the attributes of a sound and balanced assessment system.

- Understand the issues related to unethical and inappropriate use of student assessment, and protect students and staff from such misuse.[5]

School leadership within a version of the performance-based learning protocol must also be able to evaluate a student's progress in relation to and in consideration of possible academic acceleration or immediate remediation. Those decisions are made upon a series of data points, although student academic proficiency is clearly a major consideration.

Communication

The messaging around continuous assessment could use the metaphor of a Global Positioning System (GPS). Many drivers today rely on GPS to give them step-by-step instructions about which routes to take. Likewise, in order to make academic progress, a student must know where they are and how to get from there to where they want to go. The continuous assessments are an academic GPS on their journey to mastery.

Another important aspect of the assessment communication is that most of these assessments are formative, not summative. Since the formative is frequently used by the teacher to determine what the student has learned and what content needs additional work, this is not continuous high-stakes testing. Instead, it is a way for students and teachers to measure academic progress or identify possible issues for remediation.

Support

Although the use of technology for performance-based learning makes the work of grading multiple choice tests easier for the teacher, assessments are typically written to test more than simple recall. Student understanding and application of content knowledge is demonstrated in the "show your work" portion of math or in the essay and discussion questions in history or language arts. So, some of the support for continuous assessment comes in the form of the acquisition of technology. The development of a protocol and acquisition of intuitive software for data access and analysis is also crucial for the success of this aspect of the work.

Scope

This doesn't apply only to core or tested subjects. If it is the philosophy of the district that each student needs to know the progress that has been made academically at all times through affirmative testing, then the scope must be pervasive and district-wide. It doesn't make sense to know where you are in language arts but not in history.

Strategy and Reach

Placing every student in the educational environment where they will be most successful requires constant monitoring of student progress, followed by mapping to a personalized learning plan (PLP) for every student. This is not a bubble sheet or a series of test results, but a narrative about a student's strengths and weaknesses, their career preferences, and their dreams. This dossier should fully describe each student.

Timing

Conversion to continuous assessment can be a gradual process. The common assessments can occur every nine weeks, and, of course, teacher-created assessments are continuous even in most traditional programs. Writing and development of items for common assessments are both time-consuming and resource consuming. Ideally, you would have a continuous common assessment in place for each course every nine weeks or more frequently, but that may not be feasible initially.

Continuum

Progress may be slow, particularly in the development of common assessments. But since the bulk of the need is for formatives, and not necessarily summatives, much of the continuous assessment is done through regular teacher-devised check-ins (tests, quizzes, bell ringers, etc.).

The follow-through for continuous assessment is to have enough reliable data to be able to use the formatives as leading indicators.

Staffing

Smaller districts may not have a full-time administrator who is exclusively assigned to testing or accountability. The executive in charge of compliance and testing might have a variety of other responsibilities. Like much of the work in the district, continuous assessment and data analysis can be a cooperative effort. Members of professional learning communities and school administrators all participate and contribute.

Of course, a district administrator must own the ultimate responsibility because compliance with state and national testing requirements is the issue here. There needs to be a single source of contact for issues like testing irregularities when it comes to common assessments.

Assessment and Analysis

In this age of accountability, there is a tendency to create a so-called balanced scorecard with twenty pages or more of targets to meet. Most of these key process indicators (KPIs) are lagging indicators and are reported on an annual basis. Scorecards that are tallied even on a monthly basis are a difficult management tool.

What's most important? Is there a way to create a leading indicator for what is important and monitor it weekly? Reduce the number of KPIs to a handful and focus on leading indicators to be frequently monitored. If it takes more than one page to list your KPIs, you have too many.

A highly regarded math and science coordinator in a district in North Carolina was asked in a March meeting with executive staff if the students were going to make their targeted academic outcomes. She proceeded to present everything that she had done differently from the year before that should have made a difference, but never really answered the question. Much to her dismay, she did not make her targets. Continuous assessments would have provided her with some leading indicators. Her guess would have been truly "educated."

Even real-time data is not perfect, but it's better than the annual numbers that are published after the students are gone for the summer (or often after they return in September). Comparing the data from the formative assessments that occur through the year with the end-of-year summative assessments will also allow teachers to adjust instruction for the accuracy of the formatives.

For example, if the formatives indicate a better result than the summatives, then increase the rigor of the formatives to more closely align the results. If the opposite is true (lower formatives, higher summatives), it is still best to adjust the rigor of the formatives so that the teachers can use the results as leading indicators. If the gap is too wide, there will be a tendency not to rely on them or to translate results too optimistically.

Logistics

Some assessment packages are available from the Internet; others may be accessed through the state education agencies. Use reviews from long-term users to determine what package or variety of packages might be useful for your specific program and content. The frequency of assessment may still mean that the daily items are created by the classroom teachers. Technology can be employed as a testing vehicle.

Mistakes

While inter-rater reliability (consistency of ratings between various teachers of the same course) may be a concern when dealing with teacher-created assessment material, it should not be an overriding factor that dismisses that form of evaluation. There may be some variation in teacher assessments and

grading, but discussion within the PLCs will tend to narrow any wide variations in the rigor and/or quality of assessments.

Some Points to Remember about Assessment and Data

- Continuous assessment is a process of data gathering. There are two types
  of assessment—formative and summative. Continuous assessments are
  formative. They measure how well a student understands content on a
  daily basis.
- Tests can be beneficial since they can boost student recall, enhance a
  student's awareness of their own mental processing, and nurture skills to
  cope with challenge.[6] Affirmative testing in support of performance-based
  curricula relies on the application of acquired knowledge to new problems
  and higher order thinking, not simple recall of facts.
- Teachers can create items for formative testing from a variety of electronic
  sources.
- Targeted professional development and local technical support for the
  educators are critical for the creation of rigorous material, the accumula-
  tion of student data from the assessments, and the analysis of that data.
- Frequent testing should be accompanied by frequent analysis. Regular
  meetings of PLCs can be useful for this.
- Instructional leaders must provide guidance so that classroom assessments
  provide decision makers with different kinds of information at different
  times and in different forms to substantiate student progress toward learning.[7]
- The purpose of continuous assessment is to develop a set of real-time data
  about the academic progress of each student. This data is used for deciding
  appropriate ongoing placement.
- Assessments are a student's academic GPS on their journey to mastery.
  Technology can be used to support this work. All content areas should be
  included in this effort, not just state "tested subjects."
- Conversion to continuous assessment and data gathering can be a gradual
  process.
- The position of testing administrator need not be a full-time position, but
  there should be a district administrator responsible for addressing issues
  like testing irregularities.
- Reduce the number of KPIs by identifying those that are leading indicators
  and can be reported frequently. Numerous targets reported on an annual
  basis are of little use for continuous improvement.
- Create leading indicators by developing a predictive correlation between
  formatives and summatives.
- Do not be too distracted by the issues of inter-rater reliability. Allow
  discussions within the PLCs to moderate the effect size.

NOTES

1. Stiggins, Rick, and Dan Duke. "Effective Instructional Leadership Requires Assessment Leadership." *Phi Delta Kappan* 90(4), 2008: 285–91.

2. Paul, Annie Murphy. "Five Ways to Help Your Child Conquer Tests, and Learn from Them." *New York Times*, October 5, 2015.

3. Williams, Lauren. "Superintendent Kelvin Adams Turns Around St. Louis Schools." *District Administration* 49(7), 2013.

4. Stiggins and Duke, "Effective Instructional Leadership."

5. Chappius, Stephen, Rick Stiggins, Judith A. Arter, and Jan Chappius. *Assessment FOR Learning: An Action Guide for School Leaders*. Portland: ETS Assessment Training Institute, 2005.

6. Paul, Annie Murphy. "Five Ways to Help Your Child Conquer Tests, and Learn from Them." *New York Times*, October 5, 2015.

7. Stiggins, and Duke, "Effective Instructional Leadership."

Part III

Methodologies

Performance-Based Learning Is Facilitated
by Innovative Methods

Chapter Ten

Program Delivery

What got you here, won't get you there.

—Marshall Goldsmith, corporate executive coach and Thinkers50 member

Richard Elmore describes the final step of an idealized school reform process that few schools achieve. The teachers and students internalize the management and monitoring of the learning process. Administrators model their own learning and "individuals are empowered to invoke the principle of reciprocity in relations around accountability for performance."[1]

What Elmore is describing is teacher and student ownership of an approach that will keep every student in school by delivering content in a way that each student learns best, frequently assessing a student's progress, responding to that progress by accelerating their learning, and creating a culture of collaboration and reciprocity.

Intent

In order to drastically improve academic outcomes, traditional classroom practice must change. Teachers and administrators should develop and refine a disruptive innovation system of student-centered education that is performance based. Student success hangs in the balance.

Changing the program delivery may also help keep students in school. Once in school, each student must be placed on a trajectory for success, whether in college or in a career or both. To be successful, each graduating student should have the skills and the knowledge to accomplish their goals in life and (at the very least) possess the ability to earn a living wage.

To date, traditional program delivery and its incremental innovations have been unable to do that. So the methods of program delivery must be expanded and diversified. Each student should have a personalized learning plan that includes information about their goals and career aspirations as well as their assessment results.

The classes the student selects need to match their career goals and adapt to their learning style. Students will likely need to begin scheduling classes for the next school year well in advance. This will give their school ample time to respond to each student's elementary, middle, and high school requests. The first step would be to document each student's requests for the coming year.

Each class offering should clearly explain the intended course content, how the program will be delivered, and by whom. Students and their families selecting the courses and delivery methods appropriate for their goals and learning styles may cause some classes to be oversubscribed. This is why the class menu should be made available early.

There are several ways to deliver content, and within those, various learning styles can be accommodated. Some students learn well in a traditional delivery environment, while others prefer the ability to pick and choose their own journey. Placement requires the administrator to counsel with a certain amount of finesse and the students and families to have a pragmatic view of the student's abilities.

Self-Determination

Internationally, self-determination refers to the rights of every nation to determine their form of government and their participation in international politics without coercion from other nations. It assumes, but does not require, a certain political maturity within the population.

Likewise, educational self-determination refers to a student's ability to establish their own goals and to be intentional, not only about what they want to learn but also in how they propose to do it. Since maturity is an essential component of educational self-determination, this is a program delivery method best suited to older students.

A rigorous application process should be designed so that those selected are most likely to succeed. In addition to demonstrating academic proficiency and consistent attendance, applicants must be required to demonstrate pragmatic self-scheduling skills and the ability to realistically assess their own progress and/or their need for assistance.

Each student in the program should be assigned a faculty member as an advisor/mentor. This individual should have a maximum caseload of twelve students. Advisors/mentors should not only know their students intentions for the academic quarter and their daily schedule, but also monitor weekly progress toward mutually agreed upon goals.

Access to online academic courses will increase the efficacy of this type of program, as will the flexibility of allowing students to learn independently from faculty and/or experts in the community.

Peer-Led Classes

Many educators have said that the deepest learning occurs by teaching. Allowing students to teach content to their peers under the guidance of a faculty member creates that opportunity for students to acquire deeper knowledge.

Instructors whose students have been given the chance to teach claim that those students never fail to give unique insights into the material. Those insights help their peers connect more easily to the content. References to people, music, or social media with which students are familiar can clarify the subject matter for them. These are often references with which the teacher may not be familiar.

Peer-led instruction has been an effective instructional tool in higher education for medical and legal content for many years. However, it is used infrequently in K–12 classrooms. Peer-to-peer collaboration appears to be the preferred methodology by far. Adherence to pacing guides and the focus on "classroom management" within teacher education programs may be influencing the use of peer-led methodologies in this case.

Virtual

Technology can give students access to online courses twenty-four hours a day, seven days a week for credit. It provides the scheduling flexibility to adapt to the issues that often cause students to mistakenly think that dropping out of school is their only alternative.

There are three issues to consider when offering a virtual alternative to traditional pedagogy—the quality of the programming to be offered, the technical support that is available on site, and administrative support available within the district.

There is a vast array of digital programming available in education. A review protocol should be developed in order to select appropriate material for your students. Unfortunately, cost and quality do not necessarily correlate in this situation. If a decision is made and the purchased material is not effective for the students, do not hesitate to work with the vendor to adjust the software to your requirements. Many vendors have the capacity to revise their product to suit local needs.

Regardless of the online-vendor support available, you will need in-house expertise as well. This person should understand your specific needs and local conditions. Technical expertise in support of instruction is necessary for the smooth operation of all components of the system.

Much of the advantage of virtual education will be lost if there is no administrator to orchestrate the program. This position can work with struggling students and give them alternatives to the traditional delivery systems that are not working for them. This individual must be delegated enough authority to make a difference.

Flipping

In a flipped classroom, the student reviews the content lesson outside of class and works on the assignments in class—homework in class and lessons at home. Hence, the term "flipped." Reliance on technology is typical of flipped classroom-delivery techniques since students must have access to lesson content outside of "class time."

One of the advantages of a flipped classroom is that teachers are able to concentrate their class time on those students who are struggling with what would be homework in a traditional setting. Many teachers allow students to work ahead or work in peer groups while the teacher does just-in-time remediation with the group that is having trouble with the content.

In a flipped classroom delivery the students are able to play and replay the lesson content. For those who take notes, it means they can replay what they did not hear the first time or replay the entire lesson for clarity or review. Just as with homework in a traditional delivery method, there will be some students who don't listen to the lesson. Address this quickly. Is this a technical problem or a recalcitrant student?

Lessons videotaped by the classroom teacher have proven to be more effective than off-the-shelf presentations of content from a vendor. The personal connection with the teacher is part of this, as well as the ability of the teacher to dramatize and personalize the lesson to make it more interesting.

Lesson content should be no longer than about twenty-five minutes. A minimum of twenty-five content lessons should be prepared prior to the school start so that those students who want to move ahead can do so.

Blended

Blended learning is useful for those teachers whose content needs to be current. What does Crimea look like in the latest world geography textbook? Probably not the same as it does on Google Earth. Blended learning is also helpful for those subjects that require continuous assessment like mathematics. Technology can keep track of a student's proficiency and also identify concepts with which the student is having difficulty.

Teachers approach blended learning in two ways. The technology can be used as a primary resource (like a textbook) or as a supplementary resource (research or practice exercises). Incorporation of digital technology depends upon the subject matter and the teacher's ability to use the tools.

Project Based

Maker spaces and project-based delivery are becoming very popular. Like teaching, seeing a practical application for the content provides deeper insight into the content. Visual learners also tend to flourish in maker spaces by being able to see and apply what they are learning.

In one variation, Community Charter School, a K–5 school in Charlotte, North Carolina, used to allow their students to select the topic for a semester from among a long list. Once selected, all of the content was taught in relation to the selected topic. For example, if the topic was the ocean, the language arts, math, science, geography, music, and art classes related to the sea.

In today's high schools, much of the project-based content is delivered through career and technical education (CTE) courses. Although the inclusion of technology into the CTE offerings has enticed some highly able students to take advantage of this program, it still carries some of the onus of its inception as vocational education and therefore appeals more to the student who is seeking a trade school career.

Requiring every student to select a career and creating a broad range of study selections, such as aviation, visual and performing arts, financial services, and forensic medicine can eliminate the stigma attached to CTE. The challenge of career readiness has allowed districts to begin training their students in communication, presentation, critical thinking, creativity, teamwork, and social proficiency needed for success after graduation.

Leadership

Leaders at each level (board, superintendent, and executive staff) must understand and agree that traditional pedagogy does not meet current needs for everyone and that changing the paradigm (rather than incrementally improving the current paradigm) is necessary in order to create an educational environment in which every student can be successful.

The board must unite with the superintendent to accomplish this, making it clear that they are relying upon the superintendent to implement the new system of diversified program delivery because it is imperative that every student succeed after graduation. The superintendent must encourage and support changes to traditional program delivery. After making it clear that this protocol will ultimately be available to the entire district, the superintendent should delegate the authority to make these changes to the executive team.

Communication

The creation of a version of performance-based education is not an easy transition for administrators or teachers, but giving students the opportunity to learn in different ways has proven to increase the chances of success for many students who are often left behind. Communication about this change and its purpose must flow both ways so that the concerns of the community, parents, and staff are heard and addressed by the district.

It is also important to convey the message that it is the intention of leadership that this change will ultimately be district-wide. This is not a pilot program for one or two schools. It will be taken to scale. Without that caveat, the effort will be viewed both internally and externally as less than serious, or something that can be avoided if one waits long enough.

Support

Support for an idea that has promise should be virtually unconditional. This is how other districts have made progress. Resources will be discussed in a later chapter, but it is understood that the public education environment operates with limited resources. However, every effort should be made to provide each teacher with the resources they need to be able to make a difference. Unfortunately, that often means prioritizing or finding alternative sources of funding.

Support is also a matter of attitude. Negativity tends to reduce creativity and lead to self-censorship. Groups like IDEO (a design and consulting firm) that are known for their innovative solutions advise that negative comments should be eliminated from discussions of new ideas, and participants should be encouraged to build upon the ideas of others.[2] District leadership should model this type of support consistently in public and private.

Consistency

The change to alternative methods of instructional delivery requires whole-hearted belief and action. Have you ever worked with someone whose views vary depending upon the audience? These are not the people who will convince others that changing program delivery is feasible and/or worth the effort. Authentic support is the only way to convince veteran staff members, who have been taken through the "next big thing" numerous times, that this is a change that will be permanent and valuable.

Every staff member interviewed should believe this is a better way to teach and that they could never return to their former classroom practices. This is attributable to the consistency of the message from district leadership.

Strategy and Reach

The logic of changing the method of program delivery is clear. The difficulty is that it initially involves more work for the teaching staff. Some districts have allowed teaching staff to transition gradually into some aspects of program delivery, not forcing a specific method of delivery all at once. Some students will learn better in the traditional format, and so you will still have teachers that prefer to teach that way.

Reaching to every level of the organization is critical with such a drastic change. Without instructional support at each school, there will be a passive-aggressive response. Every principal must be involved in the weekly professional learning community meetings to reinforce the principles of performance-based education and the inclusion of alternative delivery methods.

Staffing

Flexibility in staffing assignments is necessary to provide all the instructional support to the various delivery methods. Some, like independent study and virtual learning, need less support. Others, like instructional technology within every delivery method, may require additional staffing. Sensitivity to the requirements of each is critical to success. Work with union representatives as needed to accomplish some flexibility.

Logistics

The logistics of making the initial change to diversify program delivery are very complex, and continuous improvement will mean that instructional delivery never stands still. The initial change may begin with tools rather than methodology. It could begin with a bring-your-own-device or a one-to-one technology program. With the electronic devices in the hands of every student in certain grades, all that may be required is telling the staff what you have in mind and asking for volunteers. Again, by communicating an aspirational purpose, you may be able to secure the support of some early adopters and, within a year or so, of the rest of the staff.

Mistakes

This above all must be a thoughtful and well-choreographed effort. Do not buy the tools and then not tell the teachers what you expect, or tell the teachers what you expect but then not provide them with the resources they need. Put a trusted detail-oriented staff member in charge of this effort, one who has a track record of timely completion of complex projects. This work contains many moving parts.

Some Points to Remember about Program Delivery

- Changing program delivery is a response to the academic needs of every student and places them in the educational environment where they can do their best.
- Self-determined delivery will appeal to those students mature enough to take control of their own learning experience.
- Peer-led classes will give students the opportunity for the deeper understanding of content that comes from teaching.
- Virtual delivery increases access to academic programs and gives the district the agility and flexibility to meet each student's scheduling requirements.
- A flipped delivery gives teachers the chance to immediately address the need for remediation in a small group.
- Blended learning will introduce the benefits of modern technology into traditional delivery models.
- Project-based delivery will allow students to see practical applications for the knowledge and skills they are acquiring and permit the district to train students in skills they will need to be successful in their careers after graduation.
- This is a district-wide change and not a pilot program that will not be taken to scale. It will require the wholehearted support of district leadership and consistency of message.
- Allow flexibility in staffing assignments.
- Consistency and transparency will carry the effort.

NOTES

1. Elmore, Richard F. *School Reform from the Inside Out*. Cambridge, MA: Harvard University Press, 2004.

2. IDEO. "Design Thinking for Educators." d.school, The Hasso-Plattner Institute of Design at Stanford. 2012. http://www.designthinkingforeducators.com/ (accessed July 7, 2015).

Chapter Eleven

Accelerated Learning

Things have a momentum, and at a certain point you can't really tell whether you have created the momentum or it's creating you.

— Annie Lennox, musician

Making a child wait to learn more until all of their classmates learn the content is counterintuitive and unproductive. Accelerated learning (the ability to move through academic content at your own pace) should be offered to every student. Chronological age can still be used to determine a student's grade level, but grade level should have little to do with which classes the student is able to master.

Intent

The purpose of the acceleration is to continually increase challenges so that students develop learning momentum and never succumb to academic inertia. As knowledge and skills are acquired, more opportunities are presented. And as those are mastered, even more are made available.

The physics principle of bodies in motion tending to stay in motion are at work here. The inspiration for this change must be driven from the top. The purpose of the initiative must be clearly and consistently stated and resources provided when and where they are needed. In a zero-dropout protocol, it is important to keep students challenged, interested, and motivated.

As students demonstrate proficiency and move on to more difficult material at their own pace, their successes begin to build confidence in their ability, and their momentum becomes a strong motivator in their continued success.

While no child should be held back, a minimum threshold should also be established. "At grade level" is that minimum. This means that as soon as a child struggles with grade-level content, remediation begins. The classroom teacher is the first line of defense.

Once a deficiency is noticed, additional help should be offered immediately. This is not a waiting-to-fail environment. Instead, there should be just-in-time interventions.

When accelerated learning is put into place, there must be end-to-end destinations. If a student progresses at their own pace and is ready for sixth-grade math in third grade, there must be a way to deliver it. If a sixth-grade student is ready for trigonometry, there must be a way for them to study it. If a student has finished all the courses needed for graduation, there should be early college courses available for credit.

There are many interrelated and complex issues for a school, feeder, or district that wants to develop an accelerated-learning protocol, but happily the conversion can be phased in and accomplished gradually and not necessarily all at once.

Leaders

Students drop out of high-performing high schools, too. District leaders understand that frequently students become unmotivated because they are bored in class, held back by their chronological age or their ability to understand content in few subjects long before their peers. Because they are required to sit and listen to content they have already mastered, they either tune out or become classroom management problems.

This is one of the reasons that tracking (i.e., grouping students by ability), although controversial, has come into favor again. Accelerated learning solves that by continuously challenging students. And as the academic momentum builds, the students acquire skills and knowledge even faster.

Accelerated learning is an interrelated system of means and methods. This cannot be accomplished by one person but needs someone of influence to be the champion. It will take several staff members mapping out and solving the complications of the system. The best way is to reverse engineer the process. Begin with expanding the early college program, and work your way down through the grade levels.

Communication

The support of staff and parents will be crucial. Communication should involve both careful listening as well as delivering pertinent information. The preliminary discussions should involve purpose. Why are we instituting this change? Some parents will be concerned about the safety of their children in an educational environment with older students. Teachers will want to know about logistics, additional workload, and technical support.

Frequent and authentic communication that fully addresses each concern is necessary for success. Utilizing social media as well as print and broadcast media may be helpful, since many of your constituents receive news about the district from a variety of sources. You should create a group of "experts" to deliver the message.

These experts can be administrators or teachers. They could be the ones that have built the model. The consistency and accuracy of the message makes this a powerful tool, so internal discussion and practice prior to public unveiling are important. The most effective communication is often teacher to teacher, parent to parent and teacher to parent.

Support

The decisions about accelerating individual students don't belong on the superintendent's desk. These are decisions that are made at the school level by the teachers and administrators, consistent with a protocol that has been developed, published, and vetted in advance.

Once the program is in place, anticipate that some parents, whose children are not being accelerated as fast as they would like, will complain. This is one more reason to strictly follow the established protocol with no exceptions.

Scope

What is the ultimate scale of this change you would like to make? Is it zero dropouts in an isolated elementary/middle/high feeder? Or will it eventually be taken to scale throughout the district? Will it be incorporated exclusively into an at-risk feeder? You may prefer to try acceleration in a feeder that mirrors the demographics of the district. It is also possible that you may only want to begin with one school. Regardless of where you start, you should know where you are headed. And remember, a single program alone will not produce a 100 percent graduation rate.

Strategy and Reach

A change to multiage grouping and self-pacing cannot be carried on the shoulders of the superintendent alone. A close working relationship with the school board and the initial conversion of at least a small group of influential staff is critical to beginning this work. Students, parents, staff, and the community should ultimately collaborate on this effort.

Timing

Plan how long this will take, and have a realistic target date in mind. This will allow you to schedule resource allocation and monitor progress. If your goal is a six-year conversion, and you have half of the schools involved in accelerating learning in the second year, you are doing great! If it is year five, and you still have only half of the schools involved, you need to figure out what went wrong.

Perhaps your schedule was too optimistic. Maybe the communications were just too complicated or you underestimated the resistance. In any case, a timeline for completion and progress monitoring are requirements for gauging success.

Eligibility for acceleration or remediation as established by continuous assessments must be cause for immediate action. Waiting for the semester or the school year to end is unproductive and contrary to the momentum you are trying to achieve.

Continuum

As mentioned earlier, in order for your high school students to fully benefit from acceleration, there must be a postsecondary opportunity. This is one of the positive rewards for completing the required high school coursework early.

Many local universities and community colleges are willing to work with you to develop early college-credit courses. The benefit for them is that they enroll additional students at times in the day when they have empty seats. They also benefit from establishing a relationship with students prior to graduation. The majority of students who begin taking courses at an institution tend to stay at that institution.

An initial step for an early college program could be dual-credit courses offered by college faculty at the high school. Once a working relationship is established, a more extensive partnership can be developed.

Staffing

This program will need a champion with authority. Creating an accelerated learning program in your district means the superintendent, his or her staff, and the board must provide unequivocal encouragement and support. If there is not someone with an available schedule to make acceleration a reality, a project manager should be hired to implement the program. This position should be a direct report to district leadership.

If some of your staff transfer to other schools or decide to leave the district, it will be more important to hire the new staff for attitude. It is far more difficult to change a pessimist into an optimist than it is to change a novice into an expert. (*Novice* here refers to someone unfamiliar with multi-age groupings and accelerated learning. They could be a teacher newly graduated or one that has been teaching for years.) But in order to turn a novice into an expert, the novice has to be allowed to try and fail.

Each educator is given over 180 days each school year to make a difference in the lives of their students. Hiring for attitude means that on some of those days they will fail to make any difference. The system must give them the professional safety net and staff development to gain the skills they need in order to make a difference.

An acceleration and self-pacing program will require substantial, targeted professional development. Administrators and teaching staff will need instructional reinforcement. Review student data every week as part of that process.

Assessment and Analysis

Continuous assessment and analysis is a component of this program. Each student's progress must be measured and analyzed for appropriate placement. Measures of Academic Progress (or a similar program of assessments) can be used as quarterly formative assessments, and teacher-created assessments can be used on a daily or weekly basis. Progress must be measured frequently and formally because it is important to document and share these assessments. Students must be placed on the basis of hard data, not teacher intuition or a soft evaluation.

Before starting an acceleration program, you must decide how state end-of-grade testing will be handled. Is a "fifth grader" always a fifth grader, even though he or she may be taking high school geometry? This will require accelerated students to be spiraled back for a review prior to the state testing. Once you decide how to record a student's grade level, discuss your methodology with the local state department of education. They will know if waivers may be required for what you plan to do.

Logistics

Strong partnerships with your board and your staff make acceleration possible.

Clearly, accelerating classes within a single school building is easier than moving between buildings or campuses. But eventually, the gaps between elementary and middle and middle and high school must be bridged. If the schools were located farther away from each other, a longer transition (class-change) time would be required as well as relaxed rules about being tardy to class.

This is also an environment in which each student needs access to a device. A one-to-one device environment is not required, but it does make the evaluation of student progress much easier. Additional resources will be needed for additional bus runs, technical support, and additional targeted professional development.

In a large district, all schools do not necessarily have to maintain the same schedules, but those that share students should. That means an entire feeder system (high school, middle, and elementary) will be on the same start and dismissal schedule and have the same number of periods during the school day. This will ease the burden on transportation costs but will strain schedules for district-wide school-level meetings and athletic schedules. Consider teleconferencing to ease this issue of scheduling.

Mistakes

It is necessary to understand the current concerns about high-stakes testing. For good or bad, we assess ourselves and our colleagues on a daily basis. So it's not the assessment that's the problem. It's correlation between the testing and giving every school a letter grade, evaluating teachers on how many of their students achieved proficiency, or threatening their livelihood if they are unable to develop high test scores.

Continuous formative assessment makes sense in an accelerated learning environment. The results can be used as indicators of student progress, identify the need for just-in-time remediation, and provide an opportunity to build academic momentum.

It is a mistake to believe that because of the outcry from students and parents about high-stakes testing, that all testing should be abolished.

Some Points to Remember about Accelerated Learning

- Chronological age and the speed at which an individual acquires knowledge and/or skills is not a reflection of intelligence. Grouping by chronological age is a device employed for efficiency, not effectiveness.
- Allowing a student to learn at their own pace induces momentum into the learning continuum. Academic momentum is a learning accelerant.
- A system of accelerated learning can be phased in beginning with an early college program in the upper grades.
- A system of accelerated learning should also establish a threshold (minimum).
- Just-in-time remediation should also be incorporated into an acceleration program.
- Acceleration requires the collaboration of many different aspects of instruction but should be orchestrated by a leader with access to power.

- Accelerated learning is a tool to reduce the number of students that drop out, because students who are challenged and not bored by reviewing content they've already learned tend to remain in school.
- Placing students in the best situation for them to learn means continuously challenging them and keeping them excited about learning more.
- The protocol for accelerated education must be clearly defined. Continuous assessment is used for determining eligibility.
- Formative results should not be available to the public. These are learning exercises for the students and progress measurements/leading indicators for teachers and families, not high-stakes tests.

Chapter Twelve

Just-in-Time Remediation

Failures, repeated failures, are finger posts on the road to achievement. One fails forward toward success.

—C. S. Lewis

A multilayered response to intervention (RtI) may seem to be a highly regimented and prescriptive technique of remedial instruction. And while all the steps and all the terminology might be the same, in the hands of creative professionals, students receive instruction and intervention that is timely, highly personalized, and attuned to their specific requirements.

Intent

Remediation is not the result of a fixed (how smart you are) mindset; this is strictly growth (how much can you learn) mindset material. Remember Shane Lopez's research into those that have hope and resilience? Through timely remediation, you are helping students acquire the essential tools of hope: goals, agency, and pathways. [1]

And this is not just about reteaching; there is a social component to remediation as well as an academic one. Andrew Zolli cites that in resilience research, "the ability of members from certain communities to bounce back from adversity is also aided by high-functioning social networks." [2] A caring adult can provide the social support a child needs to bounce back.

The goal is to take students testing at or below a cutoff line (e.g., the 10th percentile) and get them to a higher level (e.g., the 20th, or better still, grade level). Once they understand the content with which they have been struggling, many students continue to accelerate and move beyond their grade level.

The systematic evaluation of students' abilities and the corresponding adjustment of instructional delivery to advance those students seems like common sense. The marriage of performance-based education and RtI is a perfect match. The idea of "waiting to fail" that has characterized traditional education in the past has no place in a student-centered process that creates a variety of instructional delivery methods and places students in the best environment for them to learn.

There are teachers who may see RtI as a way to get struggling students out of their classroom and into an alternative assignment. Instead, RtI should be used to make sure students are properly placed. The same assessments that identify students that need additional help can also used to accelerate those students who demonstrate their knowledge and ability to apply it.

Assessment

Universal assessments (RtI Tier I) can be used as initial indicators of proper placement. If a student can demonstrate that they have mastered the content, they are put into the next level. If a student cannot show understanding of the content, a second assessment should be administered, and discussions with the teacher are initiated. Help can be given in the form of RtI Tier II (small-group instruction). If progress monitoring indicates additional help is required, one-on-one intensive assistance should be provided (RtI Tier III).

Only after these interventions have failed should a special education referral even be considered, and it should be specific to the issue that is causing the student to struggle. Like every other placement, special education is a differentiated assignment and should not be a category or group.

One tool that can be used for the initial screening is Measures of Academic Progress. As a minimum, they need to be given to students every six to eight weeks. Normative cut scores can be used to identify students at the top and bottom. A student who scores above the 90th percentile in a specific area can be considered for acceleration (usually to the next grade level of that content area).

A student who scores below the 10th percentile should be considered for additional evaluation. AIMSweb and other similar tools can be used for that further evaluation. The student's scores are just one indicator. Progress should also be discussed with his or her teacher as one more source of information.

An intervention team consisting of an intervention specialist, the school principal, the student's teacher, the student's parent(s), and a district executive should meet and discuss the student's placement and what interventions are appropriate. Placement is ongoing and not dependent upon a calendar milestone (end of course, end of grading period, etc.).

Once a student is placed in Tier II or Tier III for interventions, an intervention teacher should be assigned, and student progress is monitored on a weekly basis. As a rule of thumb, at any one time, about 5 percent of the elementary school students are identified as being in need of intervention.

Second Level

Tier II services should be given to students as small-group instruction, normally five students or fewer. The evidence-based interventions must be specific to the issues requiring remediation—phonics, reading comprehension, and so on. The interventions or group instructions can be administered by trained student tutors (see S.T.A.R.S. in a later chapter), or classified/certified personnel.

Third Level

Tier III interventions are given to students as one-to-one or in some cases one-to-two tutoring. These sessions should be done for a minimum of thirty minutes per day. After about eight weeks in Tier III, if there is no evidence of progress, a special education referral (specific to the deficit) can be considered.

Once a student's progress is measured at the upper-level cut score, they are no longer in need of the pull-out remediation. They have demonstrated sufficient content mastery and can return to their classrooms full time.

Leaders

"Leadership is the guidance and direction of instructional improvement." Richard Elmore admits this is a deliberately unromantic view of instructional leadership. It is intentional. He believes that a less romantic view of leadership will better serve to improve education. This adjustment toward a more pragmatic view of leadership requires a conscious shift toward distributive leadership and a clearer set of design principles to guide the practice of large-scale instructional improvement.[3]

When analyzing the tactics of twelve highly successful elementary principals, Karen Crum and her colleagues found that one common trait was the extensive use of data.[4] This is important across the entire educational spectrum, but of particular importance when it comes to remediation. Careful documentation of which specific content is causing a student to struggle is helpful both to the student and to the individual helping them.

In 2001, Linda Skrla and James Joseph Scheurich posed a theory regarding remediation. They said that low-income students and students of color are strongly affected by what they term "deficit thinking." They say it is pervasive within the school systems that they studied. It is their opinion that, whether conscious or not, superintendents in many districts assume their low-income students will not succeed.

Explanations and expectations for what is possible academically for the economically disadvantaged students of their district are "shaped by the larger deficit educational discourse that assumes these children will not succeed in school."[5]

While Skrla and Scheurich don't discuss it in this way, there is no bright line dividing attitude and belief informed by experience. If you say that every child can learn, does your inner pragmatist question that attitude? After all, a regression analysis of incomes and outcomes shows that there are very few schools or districts in the United States that have created outliers.

There are two beliefs that scuttle the best remediation, and both are related to deficit thinking. The first is based upon historical data. A student's outcomes on standardized tests in core subjects tend to correspond to family income. This leads easily to the traditional educational mindset. So in the absence of creating a different dataset, one in which so-called at-risk students perform as well or better than their more affluent classmates, trends that indicate improvement are celebrated as demonstrating progress. The goal of remediation is proficiency, not the creation of "improved" trends.

The second belief, which is equally destructive to remediation, is that because of their situation, these students should be "given a break." Grade adjustment is sometimes offered to the students simply for showing up for a remedial class, regardless of the additional learning involved. Likewise, the reputation of summer school in some districts is that it lacks the rigor of the classes during the school year.

If you believe that every child has the ability to learn, then it is your responsibility to teach them. Leadership needs to "walk the talk" and leave doubts and destructive beliefs at the schoolhouse door. Remediation involving additional time and more focus may be necessary for some students and can be effective, but a less than rigorous remedial program should not be considered acceptable.

Communication

The message about just-in-time remediation is that failure is not a permanent condition. The condition is temporary and has more to do with the way the content was initially delivered than it does with the student not being smart enough to learn the material. What is the problem? How can we fix it?

Support

The school community must collectively believe in and support remediation. Of course, classroom teachers are the first line of defense, but other professionals are there to help if a student is in serious trouble. The attitude must be that the fault lies not with the student or the teacher, but with the method of delivery. The levels of remediation are not simply a reteach using the same delivery methodology. Content must be presented in a variety of ways until the student masters it.

Scope

Although this effort is concentrated at the elementary level, every student struggles from time to time. Help should be available without stigma and easily accessed at elementary, middle, junior high, or high school.

Strategy and Reach

It is almost impossible to help someone who doesn't want to be helped. And asking for help is difficult. You think it means you are not good enough. Develop a culture of safety and collaboration in which it is not seen by students as a personal flaw to require help.

Build the social capital network within the entire school community.[6] This is similar to what social services agencies call "wraparound" services, except that it occurs internally within the school. Academic remediation is just one part of that. Support of all kinds is what remediation is really about.

Timing

The purpose of just-in-time remediation is to bring an appropriate level of assistance to struggling students when they need it and not wait for them to fail at the end of some arbitrary time increment (six weeks, end of semester, etc.).

Continuum

Let's call the students that need help the "bluebirds." "Once a bluebird, always a bluebird" is not the continuum that should be in place here. Look at remediation as another type of acceleration instead. Various students begin acceleration from different points of competency. These students are simply starting from a point that is lower than the average. Acceleration is acceleration, no matter where the starting point.

Staffing

If every student is not allowed to fail, then your hiring must be extremely thoughtful. Attitude is critical for remediation. There should be empathy, but not sympathy. There must be a growth mindset (every student has the capacity to learn) and a willingness to accept responsibility and to ask for help when needed. Jeffery Cohn and Jay Moran would tell you to hire leaders who possess integrity, empathy, emotional intelligence, vision, judgment, courage, and passion.[7] That's not a bad list for all new hires.

Assessment and Analysis

How have you assessed a deficit? How will you assess improvement? Establish the goal and the expected timeline. Assess and analyze progress every week. Adjust remediation accordingly and immediately, if the milestones are not met. This is not about throwing everyone into the deep end of the pool and seeing who can swim. Remediation is about drown-proofing the entire student body.

The dirty little secret in education assessment is that state testing usually occurs in content areas that are considered core subjects: English, math, science, and history. Music has been added in the Every Student Succeeds Act (ESSA) signed into federal law in December 2015.

These are the content areas that are tested in many states and are the basis for public comparisons between schools and school districts. It is therefore no surprise that these are the subjects for which remediation is available. If a student is struggling in what have been considered elective content (art, music, etc.), there is usually no remediation provided. What if it was available? Would we produce better artists and musicians?

Logistics

Just-in-time remediation in blended learning is somewhat easier than in the traditional classroom. Here a teacher works with a handful of students who are struggling in a specific area of content while others work with technology. Once students are referred to the intervention team, most students will work in a pull-out program for the class in which they are struggling until they have regained the goals.

Mistakes

Some teachers think that the RtI protocol will permit them to remove disruptive students from their classroom. Remediation is not a tool for classroom management and should not be used as such. Clearly, a special education designation is not something to place on a student without a significant amount of thoughtful observation and testing.

The purpose of RtI is actually just the opposite, to return the student to the classroom as quickly as possible. As soon as the student demonstrates the target grasp of content, they are celebrated and returned to their class.

Some Points to Remember about Just-in-Time Remediation

- Effective remediation is multilayered and timely and is delivered in a different format from the original content.
- Remediation is accelerated learning. Understanding the content is only half of the job. The other half is to return the student to the level of the rest of their class.
- Response to Intervention and performance-based education are a perfect marriage.
- Continuous measurement provides the data to trigger remediation. An extensive use of student data is of particular importance when it comes to remediation. You can't fix what you don't know is broken.
- Remediation and continuous evaluation is an alternative to the traditional waiting-to-fail process of end-of-grade and end-of-course testing.
- Intervention teams consisting of a specialist, the school principal, the student's teacher, and a district executive should discuss a specific student's placement and any interventions that may be appropriate.
- Deficit thinking (the belief that children of poverty will not excel or that they should be given a break due to their lack of resources or family support) is particularly destructive to effective remediation.
- Just-in-time remediation flourishes in a growth-mindset environment and stalls in a fixed-mindset environment. Support for remediation should be broad based. A culture of safety and collaboration will enhance remediation.
- RtI is not a tool for classroom management.

NOTES

1. Lopez, Shane J. *Making Hope Happen.* New York: Atria Books, 2013.
2. Zolli, Andrew. *Resilience.* New York: Simon & Schuster, 2012.
3. Elmore, Richard F. *Building a New Structure for School Leadership.* Washington, DC: The Albert Shanker Institute, 2000.
4. Crum, Karen S., Whitney H. Sherman, and Steve Myran. "Best Practices of Successful Elementary School Leaders" *Journal of Educational Administration* 48(1), 2010: 48–63.
5. Skrla, Linda, and James Joseph Scheurich. "Displacing Deficit Thinking in School Leadership." *Education and Urban Society* 33(3), 2001: 235–59.
6. Leana, Carrie. "The Missing Link in School Reform." *The Stanford Social Innovation Review,* 2011.
7. Cohn, Jeffrey, and Jay Moran. *Why Are We Bad at Picking Good Leaders?* San Francisco: Jossey-Bass, 2011.

Chapter Thirteen

Career Pathways

If you're offered a seat on a rocket ship, don't ask what seat! Just get on.

—Sheryl Sandberg, COO of Facebook

Career readiness has been a hot topic for education in recent years. In fact, a recent Google search unearthed over 5,660,000 related items.

Most versions of performance-based education allow students to move more freely at their own pace in core classes (and in many CTE [Career Technical Education] courses). The students can not only "major" in a career pathway, but also get involved in other courses related to their college/career interests, or intern in a career-related field.

Intent

Career training and exposure gives students the manual and social skills to be successful. The ability to communicate on the job, work closely with other employees, solve problems within the work environment, and satisfy customers can be invaluable tools for any career. Students who see a practical connection between what they are learning and their future career are more likely to stay in school and to be more engaged.

Possibilities

By the time they reach their junior year in high school, students could be asked to select a career pathway. Career pathways are a series of programs to provide experience in the world of work, giving you not only soft skills like public speaking and teamwork, but also the important technical skills for a specific job.

At the end of the coursework, a student is typically considered career ready if they pass a standardized career-readiness exam for their specific career or an industry certification, or satisfactorily complete a capstone project or a capstone portfolio.

The variety of career pathways is expanding exponentially. Students have been given a chance to sample careers in teaching, aviation, performing arts, graphic design, communications, visual arts, agriculture, finance, retail, culinary arts, library science, dentistry and medicine, physical therapy, law enforcement, forestry, forensics, refrigeration, auto and small engine mechanics, carpentry, masonry, cosmetology, landscaping, architecture, and various facets of technology.

Student-based enterprises are another way for students to gain real-world experience. Some districts have created all sorts of student enterprises, including satellite grocery stores, satellite banks, online auction sites, retail stores, catering businesses, auto repair and detailing businesses, print shops, graphic design services, flower shops, and technology support/repair services.

Internships at local businesses offer another opportunity for students to get experience. Many community businesses enjoy the chance to demonstrate their expertise and train future employees through a supervised internship program. Regional vocational centers and technical colleges also offer career pathways for those students interested in a trade or a specialized technical career.

A career pathway that is less frequently encouraged or supported, but nonetheless valuable, is the development of entrepreneurial skills through student start-up enterprises or micro-business incubation. Modern business literature is filled with stories of successful executives and entrepreneurs who began their careers in high school.

Of course, of far more interest to the community is that many of these businessmen and women remain in the area, building the business into a profit center complete with jobs for those in the community.

Twenty-First-Century Skills

Training and experience in a career pathway doesn't develop just a student's manual dexterity but also their social dexterity. Although rarely evaluated through common assessments, it is these skills that will ultimately propel students into success in life.

Bernie Trilling and Charles Fadel list those skills in their book, *21st Century Skills: Learning for Life in Our Times.* They refer to them as the seven C's: critical thinking and problem solving, creativity and innovation, collaboration and teamwork, cross-cultural understanding, communications and media literacy, computing and technology literacy, and career and learning self-reliance.[1]

Leaders

The leadership skills that are important to the success of these programs are entrepreneurial. Partnerships with local businesses and strong and supportive community connections are crucial for a career pathways program to succeed.

Carrie Leana's research has found that successful district leadership often involves outward connections.[2] Membership in local service organizations can give the superintendent and executive staff the chance to solidify and strengthen community connections.

Communication

The traditional messaging about career education begins with the maxim that not every student will attend college, but this inevitably makes career readiness sound like a consolation prize for those unable or unwilling to go to college. Every student must be career ready. So giving them experience and training in the skills that will make them successful, regardless of their postsecondary ambitions, makes sense.

Support

The support of the local business community is especially critical for the health and well-being of a career-pathways program. Businesses provide support through advisories, donations of equipment and technology, and internships. Carefully choose businesses that model successful career practices.

Parental support is also important since, often, the activities in which these students are involved sometimes require overnight accommodations or chaperones or just moral support in regional, statewide, or national competitions.

Scope

If you want a buffet of many options, it will require a table that is both long and wide. Many of the instructional and support staff will be involved in encouraging and creating the best chances for these high school students to experience the world of work that they will inherit in a matter of a few years. Every student should be encouraged to declare a career by their junior year and participate in the academic and hands-on environments of that career. Once again, this should be student centered with the focus on interests they identify through their personalized learning plans.

Emerson, New Jersey, superintendent Brian Gatens says we must prepare our students to work as part of today's *mobile* workforce. He feels we should focus on improving students' executive decision making, anytime/anywhere work, reading/writing, teamwork, visual communications, and interpersonal skills. "As part of your classroom work, you need to pay attention to the working world your students will be entering—and to adjust your teaching choices as necessary."[3]

Strategy and Reach

Preparation for a world of work in which many of the jobs do not currently exist is a challenge. The focus must be on the skills to be acquired and not necessarily on the specific career. In addition to the three R's, all students must now master the seven C's.[4]

Timing

This is not a complete program that is born over a summer planning season, but is instead a program that requires continuous improvement. It occurs in a series of steps to what is in most districts the "land of the less able" students. So this will be a cultural change as well as a program revision.

If every student must designate a career and take the related courses, then there no longer is a differentiator between those with college ambitions and those with career ambitions. The wider the variety of possible careers from which to choose, the less it divides the student body. Of course, an extensive program of career choices will take time to implement.

Continuum

This is a long-term commitment that follows your students after graduation and into their college and career experiences. In order to determine the effectiveness of the program, you will need to know how successful your graduates have become. If they are not doing well, how can you change your program in response?

It will also be necessary for you to define the terms of success and to maintain contact with your alumni. This is easier in a smaller district and certainly more difficult in a larger one. But staying in touch with your graduates may have additional benefits in terms of building the social capital of the district as well.

In Davidson County, North Carolina, the district's strategic plan was very specific about how they intended to add value to the community. "In order to contribute growth and prosperity to our community, we must develop and graduate highly skilled young adults. They should be excited about applying what they have learned and eager to begin careers in our county, whether immediately upon graduation from high school or upon their return after college graduation."[5]

Staffing

Teachers in the career pathways disciplines may not have a deep educational background. Those in the visual and performing arts may possess teaching credentials, but those in the industrial arts and technology areas may not.

Many states have provisions for "lateral entry" certifications for professionals in other fields who would like to teach. This may also be an opportunity to hire highly qualified part-time staff—individuals who have practiced what they teach.

Establish good working relationships with professionals in the community who will know about the technical qualifications of the candidates you are considering and consult them. They should be able to tell you if the applicant is a good fit for the technical knowledge you require and whether they have the talent to train students in their specific skill.

Assessment and Analysis

The seven C's are not "tested" subjects. If you are going to teach these skills, shouldn't you evaluate whether your students are mastering them? Since these are skills and not content, the standard assessment protocol is not as effective. Develop ways to measure your students' progress in mastering the seven C's and monitor frequently.

Assess the value and quality of your program at least semiannually. Are you giving your students what they asked for? Are they learning the essential skills to be successful in a career? What needs to change or improve? What needs to be added?

Logistics

Most districts have a career and technical education program of some form already in place. The issue is how you expand and enhance your CTE program to 1) include the entire student body and 2) include a wider variety of career options.

Highly technical programs (coding, forensic medicine, engineering, etc.) have been used by some school districts to attract academically proficient students to the careers program. The visual and performing arts inclusion into the careers also permits another segment of high school students to participate.

The retail and finance career pathways could be expanded by working with local business partners. If an early-release protocol is created, the hands-on instruction could take place at the businesses, rather than at the school site. This is an instructional program so coordination of the internship program and the curriculum is also important.

Don't forget to include the encouragement and support of start-up businesses into your career and technical education possibilities. The CTE program could function as an incubator for those start-ups.

Mistakes

The biggest mistake is doing nothing. It is true that by doing so, you won't make any mistakes, but it is also true that you and your students won't make any progress.

Some Points to Remember about Career Pathways

- In the performance-based learning process, career readiness provides a bookend to the K–12 continuum and a foreshadowing of life beyond graduation for high school students.
- All students should be encouraged to select a career prior to their junior year in high school. Experience in a career can be made available through courses on campus or at regional vocational centers, student enterprises, internships at local companies, and incubation of student and faculty start-up ventures.
- The seven C's taught through exposure to careers are the foundation of student success in life.
- Community connections facilitate a strong career-pathways program.
- This is a long-term commitment. The program can develop slowly, but once in place those career choices must remain in place.
- Define success for the program. Maintain contact with alumni in order to know what should be improved.
- Career-pathways teachers may or may not have traditional teaching credentials. Use professionals within the community or hire qualified staff part-time.
- Determine how to assess the acquisition of skills and do so frequently.

NOTES

1. Trilling, Bernie, and Charles Fadel. *21st Century Skills*. San Francisco: Jossey-Bass, 2009.

2. Leana, Carrie R. "The Missing Link in School Reform." *The Stanford Social Innovation Review*, 2011.

3. Gatens, Brian. "How Teachers Can Prepare Students for the New Mobile Workforce." Concordia University. August 24, 2015. http://education.cu-portland.edu/blog/principals-office/teachers-students-new-mobile-workforce/ (accessed August 28, 2015).

4. Trilling and Fadel, *21st Century Skills*.

5. "Davidson County Schools Strategic Plan." Davidson County Schools. October 2014. http://www.davidson.k12.nc.us/UserFiles/Servers/Server_81593/File/Superintendent/SP.

Part IV

Programs

Student-Centered Programs Engender Success

Chapter Fourteen

Early College

Early college designs enable students to create and fulfill postsecondary aspirations.

—Rennie Center for Education Research and Policy, Boston, Massachusetts[1]

Accelerated learning requires attention to detail at both ends of the spectrum. A program that allows students a sample of college courses for credit also gives the district an exclamation point at the one end of the acceleration process. If your accelerated learning program is working well, many of your students will finish their required courses by the end of their second year in high school. Early college is the next academic challenge for students that have academic momentum.

Intent

Those students enrolled in an early college program are far more likely to succeed, both in college and in a career. It makes sense that the early college program be widely available, not just to those students who are highly able but to all students.

One Version

Many districts have used early college programs to reward students with high grade point averages and the maturity to handle college courses. The district may be given classrooms at the local community college or university, and a handful of students get the chance to take college courses as well as finish any required courses for high school graduation.

This creates a remarkable, elite, and usually very small high-performance school. Perhaps it may give the district a school that will compete academically in a favorable way with area charter and private schools, but it doesn't maximize the power of an early college program.

Another Version

There should not be one simple program, but a variety of them. Students might be able to take college courses online. Some dual-credit courses can be offered at the high school. Some students may prefer to attend a class at the local community college or university. And still others may be ready for a full-time college experience.

Why is this a better alternative? Because early college exposure in high school gives all students a chance to see that they can be successful in a postsecondary environment. Access to college programming keeps some students interested in school who would otherwise drop out. Keep in mind, not every dropout is a struggling student.

Early college students are more likely to enroll in college after graduation from high school and are more likely to attain a postsecondary degree. Early colleges are particularly useful in closing the achievement gap. "Early Colleges appeared to mitigate the traditional educational attainment gaps between advantaged and disadvantaged students."[2]

Leaders

The issues for district leadership are first and foremost to negotiate the best deal for your students in regard to an early college program with a local or regional postsecondary institution. And second, to make the program accessible to the broadest possible range of students. In this way, you are truly addressing the success of your graduates. This is a program that makes many of your students, many of whom do not think of themselves as "college material," begin to think an associate's or bachelor's degree may be possible.

The leadership of the district must be comfortable with unsupervised students driving to and attending the local university or community college. College presidents must also be comfortable with younger students on their campus. It is probably not the best welcoming expression for a campus leader to say that "those kids" are the source of 80 percent of the trouble on the campus. Understand what issues you will face, and be prepared by having a risk-management plan in place.

This could be a potential savings for the district. Depending upon how the resources are distributed, you may be paid on a per student basis and have fewer students to teach because they are attending the university or community college.

This also is an integral component of the accelerated learning program. It is difficult to get students motivated about completing as many credits for high school graduation as they can in their first years if there is nowhere to go in their last two years.

Communication

This is not a "Mom and Dad can save a lot of money" program. They probably will, but when pitched that way, all of the college-bound students will enroll, and none of the students who would not consider college as an option will enter the program. Instead, communication should focus on the program as a way to get college experience while you are in high school and to explore potential career options.

Support

One reason for the tremendous success of early college is that those students that take advantage of the program would still use the support mechanisms available to them as high school students. This, as well as the ability to take a limited number of courses and concentrate on them, helps students transition to college and gives those who thought they could not succeed in a postsecondary environment the success and confidence to try.

Scope

Many school districts have begun early college programs for their high school and some for accelerated middle school students. Either through intention or coincidence, these programs tend to attract the more proficient students.

It is the students who have been traditionally underrepresented in postsecondary education who actually benefit more from an early college program. Early college experiences can be especially valuable for students who do not think of themselves as college bound.

In their policy briefing on early college programs in Massachusetts, the Rennie Center for Education Research and Policy cite research that students of color and those from economically disadvantaged backgrounds are much more likely to have a successful postsecondary experience than peers who have not participated in early college.

"Ultimately, in addition to increasing college readiness and completion rates, early colleges have the potential to increase the size and diversity of the college-going population."[3]

Strategy and Reach

As part of a package that includes accelerated learning, virtual education, and career instruction for all students, early college can help those students who would otherwise convince themselves that they are not "college material" that success in higher education is feasible. In an age when high unemployment seems to be systemic among the undereducated, a two- or four-year degree is essential to earning a living wage.

That said, if the lifelong success of your graduates is the mission of your district, then the reach for the early college program must be deep and wide. This goes beyond identifying the college from which each staff member graduated and other superficial encouragements for students to consider a postsecondary experience. This is getting every student to try a college course in the safety of the high school environment and coaching them for a positive outcome.

The OneGoal program in Chicago is a companion program to consider for those students unable or unwilling to consider college as an option. In his book *How Children Succeed,* Paul Tough says, "OneGoal is a most valuable intervention, a program that, for about $1,400 a year per student, regularly turns underperforming, under-motivated low-income teenagers into successful college students."[4]

This program is not a cram course for good test scores, but a course that coaches students in how to succeed in college. It includes simple ideas like sitting up front in the class, using the time that professors schedule to be in their office to get extra help, and developing other soft skills that cause less mature students away from home for the first time to fail in college.

Timing

Early college is a program that can require some advance planning and negotiation with postsecondary institutions in your area. Once the requisite logistics are in place, the program can begin. It can start small and build to scale as the experience increases.

Continuum

Early college is a long-term experience for many students. It cannot be a program that exists one year and is eliminated the next. Consistency is critical to success since a student's further education tends to be planned in advance and based upon programs available.

Staffing

The early college program needs a champion, someone who has the leverage to eliminate barriers. This position does not need to be full-time, but available when needed for solving problems.

Assessment and Analysis

In 2014, the American Institutes for Research (AIR) released a report from their study of a random sample of ten early college programs with the following conclusions:

- Early College students were significantly more likely to enroll in college than comparison students.
- Early College students were significantly more likely to earn a college degree than comparison students.
- Early College impact generally did not differ by subgroup, and when the impact differed, the difference was generally in favor of underrepresented groups.[5]

Those "underrepresented groups" were minority, low-income, and first-generation college-going students.

These are advantages that must be distributed among the student body and not simply reserved for those highly able students who are likely to enroll and be successful in college regardless. To make sure the results were randomized, AIR selected early college programs that used a lottery system for admission to at least a portion of the available seats.

Logistics

Consider a different approach. The Early College High School program in the state of Texas is targeted at those students at risk of dropping out of high school or at risk of not graduating from college. "The program provides student support systems, including tutoring, counseling, and mentoring while reducing barriers to college for students who might not otherwise achieve post-secondary success."[6]

Many postsecondary institutions have times in their schedules that are difficult to fill. This is often during regular school hours (sometimes morning, sometimes afternoon) when a class is easy to fit into a high school student's schedule. Work with the campus administrator to identify a time that works best for them.

Negotiate a lower tuition cost for your students. However, there still may be some students who want to take advantage of the university classes but are unable to afford them. Make arrangements for those students to get a postsecondary experience, too. Sponsorships from local businesses or scholarships through various means could be viable options.

Some districts negotiate for classroom space at the community college or university and have district staff teach the core curriculum at that location. This limits access because most postsecondary institutions do not have surplus classroom space throughout the school day. These programs tend to be offered to the more able students. Some even have GPA requirements for attendance.

New technology has put the traditional postsecondary education market under attack. MOOCs (massive open online courses), for-profit online courses and degrees, and small satellite campuses for working professionals have all reinvented the traditional residential college experience. If local resources are not available, consider using virtual college programs as a substitute. Negotiation with a for-profit entity may be more challenging, but nonetheless can also be an option.

Course selection will vary student to student. Many students will use early college to eliminate some of their core requirements (math, English, social studies, etc.). Others will use early college to sample a possible career choice. Reinforce the correlation between the student's individual learning plan and the courses selected.

Mistakes

The transition from high school to college is a difficult one for the majority of students. They are completely responsible for regularly attending class, understanding the material delivered in class, and studying for their tests and course exams.

The more responsibility a student is given in high school, the more prepared they will be for the postsecondary transition. Don't abandon these students. Offer them a chance to get support when they are struggling. Because they are far more familiar with the system of support at their school, they are far more likely to seek help there. Give them that opportunity.

Many districts believe that once their students are in college, the district's responsibilities are over and assume the same is true for early college, too. It is a mistake to treat this program as a "stepchild" and ignore the needs of these students. Early college students that are given appropriate support can be exemplars of the best the district can offer.

Some Points to Remember about Early College Programming

- Early college is the perfect end point to accelerated learning. Access to postsecondary programming should be as open as possible. An elite program for those students who are high achievers does not maximize the benefits of the program.
- A buffet of early college opportunities increases availability. Virtual, dual-credit, single classes at the college/university or a full class load at the college/university are all possibilities.
- A dialogue between the leader of the district and the leader of the community college or university is necessary. This discussion should provide an

affordable way for your students to attend college. The cost of tuition is sometimes a barrier. A lower tuition removes that barrier.

- Taking college courses in high school allows the students to receive the additional support they need, limit the workload by taking one or two courses, better understand the personal and time management of postsecondary requirements, and be successful in small increments.
- Once begun, continuation and consistency of the program are important. There is nothing more disheartening to a student than to enroll in a program that changes or is terminated before their graduation.
- The early college program needs a champion who is a problem solver. This may not be a full-time position, depending upon the caseload and the size of the district.
- Work with the local colleges and universities to fully utilize their faculty. There are often blocks of time during the day (depending upon the demographics being served) that are less popular for adult students, and those offer a potential opportunity to schedule early college classes.
- Create a process in which payment of tuition is not a barrier to a higher education experience. Negotiate lower fees. Work with local businesses to sponsor scholarships.
- In the absence of a local alternative, work with a for-profit virtual provider.
- Course selection varies with each student. Some use early college as a career sampler, others use it to get core credits. Alignment to their personalized learning plan should be verified.

NOTES

1. "Early College Designs: Achieving College- and Career-Readiness for All." Policy Brief, Boston: Rennie Center for Education Research and Policy, 2015.

2. Berger, Andrea, Lori Turk-Bicakc, Michael Garet, Joel Knudson, and Gur Hoshen. "Early College, Continued Success: Early College High School Initiative Impact Study." Washington, DC: American Institutes for Research, 2014.

3. "Early College Designs."

4. Tough, Paul. *How Children Succeed*. New York: Houghton Mifflin Harcourt, 2012.

5. Berger et al., "Early College."

6. "Overview of Early College High Schools in Texas." Texas Early College High School. 2015. http://www.txechs.com/what_is_echs.php (accessed August 14, 2015).

Chapter Fifteen

Student Ambassadors

When people ask where I studied to be an ambassador, I say my neighborhood and my school.

—Andrew Young, former U.S. congressman and United Nations ambassador

A version of performance-based learning is always student-centered. A student-centered program always needs input from those students. A student ambassador program provides the board, the administrators, and the visitors with a student point of view (often missing in the typical school tour), and this kind of program allows the district to identify, coach, and reward its high-potential students.

Purpose

Every organization needs to cultivate their high potentials. Identifying this group of students across all grade levels and allowing them meaningful participation in the life and business of the district is the purpose of the program. The benefits are that these students receive training and experience in the skills that are necessary for postsecondary and career success, and the district is able to get unvarnished input about the student experience.

The program can be done by feeder schools (elementary, middle, high) in a large district, or district-wide in a smaller one. It could be started in just one school, although its effect is diminished if it is not a program available to all levels.

The student ambassadors program should be a group of about twenty-five students from grades three through twelve that represent the school district in many of its public functions. They are the hosts and hostesses at the board meetings, not only greeting attendees and handing out agendas but also presenting to the board when it is their turn to serve and offer a student's perspective.

Harding Senior High School in St. Paul, Minnesota, uses its fifty student ambassadors to bring on board transferring students. They found that the number of students transferring justified a "buddy system" that gives the new student an opportunity to learn the school from a student perspective. "The Student Ambassadors are invited to participate in the program by their teachers and counselors because they have proven to be positive, responsible, respectful students."[1]

This group should function as student advisors to the superintendent, meeting regularly with him or her and sharing their point of view on issues as wide ranging as new educational programs to designs for the new schools to be built.

As tour guides for visiting school-district personnel and education professionals, these students can offer the customer a perspective that is often overlooked and yet is so important. As hosts and hostesses for visiting dignitaries, these students provide a refreshing counterpoint to the usual social small talk.

As envisioned, student ambassadors would be selected from elementary, middle, and high school. Once selected, they would serve until they graduate. This is a select group with high potential, so the number should be kept at around twenty-five students.

Since student ambassadors would serve until they graduate, the annual selections would be based upon the number of student ambassadors graduating in a specific year. The selection process could begin with an extensive written application and staff recommendation. Candidates could then be interviewed individually and in groups in a daylong process. Numbers rather than real names should be used. In that way, the selection committee is less likely to be influenced by a candidate's family or administration connections.

This program should use every opportunity to train its students to be successful. Students should practice and role-play, learning how to field difficult questions, think on their feet, and converse politely at dinner.

They will need to understand that communicating with district visitors is different from communicating with teachers or classmates. When the superintendent asks their opinion of a change in program being considered, they can be candid but respectful.

They should be taught how to "code switch" their speech and mannerisms between lunch with their classmates and lunch with a visitor from another district. Obviously, when speaking to a visiting state senator, they are clearly more formal and perhaps somewhat less candid than they are when speaking to their friends.

This code-switch training should be a feature of many of the programs. Students will learn that their words, actions, and even their attire should change based upon the situation. They can be taught the appropriate attitude and vocabulary for job interviews and college applications. Whether it is the S.T.A.R.S. (see chapter 16), the student ambassadors, or the students in the career-pathways program, they will be mastering these skills.

While student ambassadors could be a very popular program in your district, it cannot be a popularity contest. Students should be selected for their potential, not necessarily their ability to represent the school district on their first day as student ambassadors. The extensive interview process must include evaluating students on attitude and potential.

Although there should be certain academic limitations for participation in a student ambassador program regarding grade-point averages, the program provides an opportunity for students of all socioeconomic levels to demonstrate leadership as well as get training and life experience in skills such as public speaking and social interaction across various social strata, skills that are certain to increase a student's likelihood of career success.

Districts have found all sorts of ways to include students in the business of the district. The board at Anne Arundel County Schools in Maryland seats a voting student board member every year. That member is elected through the Chesapeake Regional Association of Student Councils (CRASC). Many districts have created student advisory committees for the superintendent. Budget advisory committees often include students. Create meaningful ways to include your students in your business activities.

Leaders

In order to make the student ambassadors program successful, district leadership should provide opportunities for these high-potential students to participate in the business of the district—board meetings, visits by dignitaries, superintendent advisories, and more. Having a committed staff member, a champion, for this program is critical.

Communication

This is a prestigious group of students. Selection cuts across all schools and all grades. It is neither a popularity contest nor a chance to pick the rich and famous. As envisioned, the ambassador program will provide student representation to all important events in the district and provide student input and viewpoint to visitors and district staff.

Support

Parents and staff need to support the program. The younger students will need transportation to and from events, and all of the ambassadors are asked to serve at times during school days, so teachers are asked if the absence will be disruptive.

Student ambassadors also need the support of district staff for training and scheduling, and they need the support of the superintendent and the board. This is not a ceremonial position. It is a position that is supposed to provide a heretofore unheard viewpoint to decision makers. If that advice is not heeded or is dismissed as nonconsequential, the program will suffer.

Monetary support will also be required from time to time. The student ambassadors should wear a simple uniform such as a polo shirt and khaki slacks. The uniforms can be purchased by the district. They also need support for transportation to and from training, if the training occurs off-site.

Scope

While the program has a district-wide footprint, it is a program for twenty-five students. One district employee is needed to schedule events, develop training exercises, and create/facilitate the selection process.

Strategy and Reach

The idea for the program is to provide a student presence and input into the business of the district and, by doing so, train the students in the twenty-first-century skills they will need to be successful. These will tend to be students who have an interest in politics, communications, public relations, and hospitality careers. So in addition to the skills training and the notoriety of being an ambassador, they will get some on-the-job experience in communications and hospitality.

These students are trained as district representatives. Consider how to best use their expertise. Could they attend PTA/PTSO meetings? Can they be included in the formulation of school improvement plans? Will their input be of benefit to state legislators on education issues?

Timing

This is a program that takes very little time to implement. Students can apply for open positions in the spring. They can be selected prior to the end of school. They should receive training during the summer and then begin their service during the next school year. As the continuity is important, ambassadors should continue to serve until they graduate from high school.

Continuum

These high-potential students not only become the student leadership of the district but also the ones to watch from every graduating class. These are the active alumni that will continue to be connected to the district through reunions, fundraisers, and homecomings. They are the core of your community support from the next generation.

Staffing

One district staff person will need to take responsibility for the group. This is not a full-time job, but an important one. The person who fills this position should have a better than average track record for identifying high potentials and be able to model and teach the necessary soft skills to students at all grade levels.

Empathy and authenticity are required for this position. Without those strengths, this person will not be able to develop the reciprocal trust and respect from the students necessary to guide this program successfully.

Assessment and Analysis

Because many of the results of the program are behavioral and interpersonal, evaluation of the program will tend to be subjective. Make expectations clear. Evaluate in close proximity to the event (after-action reports). These evaluations don't need to be extensive. The group should identify one or two things that could be improved and several others that were successful.

Logistics

This is a fairly simple program to put into place. Secure board support, find a funding source for the training and the simple uniforms, and identify logical points of inflection in the business of the district where student participation would be beneficial. Create a selection criteria and a way to evaluate candidates anonymously. Announce the program and seek applications. Celebrate the new student ambassadors!

Mistakes

In working with this group of students, there must be a loose/tight balance. Too tight a grip on the reins will limit the input and the enthusiasm from the individuals. They are young and inexperienced and will likely say some things you wish they had not said. Try not to overreact. Remember your culture should be a safe place to make mistakes. Acknowledge the occurrence and move on.

Some Points to Remember about a Student Ambassadors Program

- Performance-based education is student centered. A student ambassadors program allows the district to identify and coach its high-potential students as well as get input.

- A student ambassador program can be done school by school or district-wide. All levels should be represented.
- Selection process should be rigorous and anonymous. Selection should cut across socioeconomic lines.
- Student ambassadors learn social competence as a result of their service.
- This is a program that is easy to implement and can be done fairly quickly.
- This program could supply the core of the district's community support from the next generation.
- Assessments of the program should consist of after-action reports that identify improvements that can be made and successes.
- Student ambassadors need to be recognized. Most programs use a simple uniform.

NOTE

1. "Student Ambassadors." Harding Senior High School. 2015. http://harding.spps.org/student_ambassador_program.html (accessed December 4, 2015).

Chapter Sixteen

S.T.A.R.S.

I have come to believe that a great teacher is a great artist and that there are as few as there are any other great artists. Teaching might even be the greatest of the arts since the medium is the human mind and spirit.

—John Steinbeck

The S.T.A.R.S. program (Students Teaching and Reaching Students) was originally conceived as a program to give high school juniors and seniors the chance to experience the thrill of teaching. It complements the versions of performance-based education and gives students a chance to understand that teaching isn't all that easy.

Intent

Use this program to teach students "life lessons." S.T.A.R.S. learn to be punctual and reliable because others are counting on them. For example, a student who is assisting in the school office by telephoning each absent student begins to understand not only the importance of attendance but also the importance of giving the office the correct emergency-contact information. The second or third time they telephone "dial-a-prayer" because that is the emergency contact information listed in the student's records, they begin to wonder what would happen in a serious emergency.

There are several reasons why you might want to begin a program like S.T.A.R.S.:

- Responding to the interests of your students;
- Reducing the workload for teachers;
- Growing your own teaching corps;

- Preparing your students for careers;
- Connecting students with community businesses;
- Utilizing student expertise with technology;
- Assisting struggling students with cross-age and peer tutoring; and
- Enhancing program delivery by including student participation.

Competency-based learning requires that students eventually gain enough maturity to begin to manage their own educational journey. This program gives students the same kind of freedom/responsibility that was previously given to the "audiovisual" kids back in the dark ages.

The audiovisual kid was given the responsibility of walking down the hall to the media center, signing out the projector and cart, bringing that equipment back to the classroom, and setting it up so that the teacher could show a movie or a filmstrip to the class.

Sometimes the equipment was stored in a separate locked storage room, and the student was also entrusted with the key to that room (often a master key). In many cases, this was an infrequent occurrence at best. These were the students who could be counted on.

Unlike the "audiovisual" kids who had infrequent responsibilities, the S.T.A.R.S. students have regular duties to perform. These students may be tutors, teacher's assistants, receptionists, lab assistants, and technology-support technicians. Often, they save the district thousands of dollars while gaining invaluable experience in the process.

This is another element of performance-based education; this is not a freelance program. It is one that is monitored and administered by staff. It happens to be hands-on training rather than content work, but it can be just as important for student success. Staff who administer the program must review and approve applications, assign students to tasks, review expectations with students and supervisors, and regularly check on progress.

Some programs have also included an apprenticeship program in which students work at jobs in the community. Similar to a co-op or early release program, this work also includes the same involvement from the administrator to verify that the goals and expectations are being met.

Selection

Students applying for the program should be given a series of essay questions. They must have multiple teacher references as well as a good record of attendance. A personal interview should be the final step in the selection process.

Above all, students must have the maturity to be of value to their supervisors. These are self-actualized individuals. Those that are teacher assistants are functioning in the place of classified staff. This is an opportunity to give the best and brightest a chance to sample the teaching profession. Those who are functioning in administrative positions are relied upon for smooth operation of the offices in which they serve. Those students that are in internships are not only learning about a potential career but also representing the district to the community.

Teaching Assistants and Tutors

This is an opportunity to couple a dual-credit, early college class in education fundamentals with this aspect of the S.T.A.R.S. program. The more information students are given about the teaching profession, the better equipped they are to be successful in it.

Although much of today's teacher shortage has been attributed to lack of substantial wages, one other reason novice teachers leave the profession is that they are unaccustomed to the requirements of the position and feel they receive little or no support once hired. S.T.A.R.S. students get two years of supervised classroom experience, much more than university students who are traditional education majors.

Those districts that are able to afford all of the teacher assistants they would like are dwindling. Many have been forced, through budgetary cuts, to limit their classified staff to the lower grades or to eliminate these positions completely. Having the S.T.A.R.S. students serve as teacher assistants is beneficial to the teachers to whom they are assigned as well as to the students that participate.

For example, using these students in the lower grades allows frequent monitoring of progress of the students, and some issues related to students struggling with the basic skills can be identified and addressed. This is especially important in areas like reading proficiency, which is one of the key ingredients for mastery in every content area.

The State of Louisiana has a S.T.A.R. (Students Teaching and Reaching) program in fifty high schools across the state. Juniors and seniors in high school can take a course, in many cases for dual credit, that gives them an overview of a career in teaching.

Some districts also use students in this program as peer-to-peer tutors or as cross-age tutors. One assistant principal related the story of a young man, who as a fifth grader in elementary school, was assigned to tutor a handful of second graders in reading. Not only did the reading proficiency of the young students improve, but the assistant principal also saw that the young man also became substantially more proficient in reading. As many educators know, teaching is another way of learning deeply.

Technical Support

Students always find it much easier to get help from other students. It is less intimidating to go to another student for help. That is particularly true of technical support. S.T.A.R.S. are particularly useful for assisting others with hardware and software issues. Chances are, they have encountered similar problems and can quickly work through to a solution. This does take a certain amount of trust on your part, but it can be a tremendous benefit to staff and students.

Administrative Positions

Many high schools use some of their students as volunteer assistants in the main office and as receptionists in the counseling offices. This is a way to give the more mature students an opportunity to help the school. However, these programs are rarely monitored. These students answer the phones and perform minimal administrative duties like running copies or issuing tardy slips, but often do so without a formal process of progress monitoring or evaluation.

The S.T.A.R.S. program puts this work in an entirely different context. This is in effect another class for these students. They are required to independently apply skills and knowledge in the workplace (albeit in-house) setting. Students are placed with on-site professionals who manage their workload and oversee their performance much as an administrator in an actual employment setting would. Additionally, a program administrator should visit the student two to three times during the year to evaluate their progress and performance.

Internships

Placement into internships is directly related to what a student identifies as his or her interests on their application to the program. The program director is responsible for seeing that these students acquire the skills necessary for a successful career—interviewing, dealing with people, wearing the appropriate attire, punctuality, reliability, and so on. They should understand the value of service to the community and to the school.

From the internship program, the employer should receive a packet of information outlining expectations. An informal follow-up can occur every two weeks or so with a formal observation about every nine weeks. Clearly, out-placement to community employers is handled very carefully since it is in the program's best interest to maintain a continuing partnership with these local businesses. Most of the students placed in internships are serious about the careers in which they intern and continue to pursue that career after the internship experience.

Leaders

Hands-on leadership is critical to the success of a program like this. A self-actualized, creative, and organized individual is needed to begin and continue the program. What the superintendent provides is unconditional encouragement and support for the mission, not a day-to-day to-do list.

Being a director for a program of nearly two hundred students is a full-time job. The administrative duties are substantial—approving applications, getting to know the students and the employers well enough to create productive placements, following up every two weeks, and then adding a formal visit and report every nine weeks. And since this program is only available to high school students, it is cyclical and must start again in January so that you are ready for input into scheduling.

Communication

The S.T.A.R.S. program was created to recognize teaching potential in students and to nurture that potential by thoughtfully placing them into situations to gain valuable experience. Some students who have identified a different career path are placed in administrative or internship roles where they, too, can gain work experience.

Support

Connections to the community are essential to the success of the schools and of this program. While it will be tempting to utilize the resources of large corporate organizations in your community, it may be more productive to connect with small businesses in the immediate area. These entities do not have access to "summer help" during the school year, and often are in need of part-time talent. They are usually willing to train and supervise an intern.

The other reason that placements to local connections are important is that your high school students must be able to get to these internships. A long commute tends to defeat the purpose of the internship. The workday is almost over before the student arrives. The program director must network in order to discover potential opportunities for placement in the immediate area.

Scope

Decide how many students your program should serve, and plan accordingly. A total caseload of three hundred is probably all a single staff member will be able to handle. The solution in a large district might be to create a separate program for each high school.

Strategy and Reach

Begin with your purpose. Then build a program around that purpose. A program that includes two hundred students will provide almost nine hundred hours of service per week to the district. That is a powerful force for accomplishing a goal.

During those nine hundred hours, the students in the program acquire the work ethic and maturity that they will need to be successful career professionals. The students they teach and tutor acquire far more.

Timing

Rather than trying to tackle everything at once, it is probably better to start by creating a program that addresses one specific need. Clearly, a program designed primarily to save the district money will look different from a program to prepare students for careers. A program to entice students into the teaching profession will look different from a program that is responding primarily to student interests. But any program you design will also have collateral benefits. School districts, both large and small, can begin this program within one high school and expand as staff and resources allow.

Continuum

The S.T.A.R.S. program might exist to return graduates to the district as educators already familiar with performance-based education. It might provide an opportunity for high school seniors to avoid inertia (senior slump), help fellow students achieve, and give valuable service to their school district. It might help students acquire the soft skills necessary for career readiness. And it can be one more opportunity on the accelerated-learning continuum.

Staffing

The unusual nature of the program results in the need for a director with unique skills. The chances of finding someone with extensive experience in this field in the available labor pool are slim. Someone who knows the students and the staff and will use that knowledge of the district's and community's needs to create a highly respected and successful program is who you are looking for. A combination of knowledge and sensitivity will make a program like this function smoothly.

Assessment and Analysis

Teachers and intern supervisors can give you feedback on whether or not the placements are working out. Try to evaluate on a biannual basis (too early, not enough information; too late, the program may suffer). Try to check with the employers by phone and the teachers in person on a monthly basis, nothing in depth, just a check-in.

Logistics

Russell Yates, educational-programming director and multiage teacher at the Swan School, in Port Townsend, Washington, offers the following guidance on Edutopia.org about starting a peer-to-peer tutoring and mentoring program like S.T.A.R.S.:

- Teach students to understand that other students do not learn by just giving them the answer. Model effective tutoring by demonstrating methods and allowing students to practice them.
- All students can be a peer mentor, not only those the teacher thinks are capable or those with high test scores.
- Pair students in your class with another, probably younger, single-grade class for peer mentoring.
- Small-group peer mentoring is like a jigsaw puzzle. The teacher gives a multipart assignment with each student in the group learning a part and then teaching that part to the other students.
- In small-group learning, employ the three-before-me rule: Students must ask for help from three classmates before raising a hand to ask for help from the teacher. This approach gives a lot of students the chance to help instruct.
- Small-group learning gets loud. To keep the noise level lower, check out Multiage-Education.com on tips for helping young students learn to control their voices. Also, print out and post the site's noise-meter poster and use as a visual reminder about appropriate voice levels. Or, create your own version.
- Peer mentoring should be used often enough to develop routines, but not so often that students lose enthusiasm for it. Try a weekly session to start.
- Each student possesses different skills. Use peer mentoring as a chance to support the development of leadership skills among all of your students. A student who struggles with reading and writing but excels in art could probably benefit from a self-confidence boost. On an art project, pair this student up with a peer who is better in the core subjects.
- Try to create a situation that benefits all students. This will make the mentoring experience genuine. When pairing students, consider their strengths and weaknesses. Be sure the exercise will benefit both students.
- Simply having students read to one another isn't as powerful as having them teach each other a specific skill. [1]

A seven-period day shared by all three levels is helpful when trying to schedule peer tutoring and mentoring across the grade levels. Block schedules are a little more difficult (because elementary schools are normally not block scheduled), but they are still workable. Consider aligning schedules (at a minimum, school start and end) at the participating schools in order to facilitate scheduling.

The logistics for the internship programs will be similar to an early-release program that many high schools use for juniors and seniors who have afternoon jobs. Be aware that many of the off-campus positions will require the student to have transportation. Equity of opportunity will be an issue if some arrangement cannot be made for those students that do not have their own transportation.

Mistakes

The logistics for this program are similar to any internship program. The challenges come by way of the cyclical nature of the program and the need to constantly identify additional opportunities. There will be some students who become "fallen S.T.A.R.S.," but the director's careful selection, coaching, and continuous monitoring will tend to limit those to a handful each year.

Some Points to Remember about Students Teaching and Reaching Students

- Students in S.T.A.R.S. act as teacher assistants, lab assistants, receptionists, and technical-support technicians. Others can participate in internships in local businesses.
- The position of director is full-time for a two hundred-student program. A caseload of three hundred is likely the maximum for one individual.
- S.T.A.R.S. is another chance for you to demonstrate that you are listening to your students and creating the opportunities and practice they need and want.
- A program of two hundred S.T.A.R.S. students can provide over nine hundred hours of service per week to the district.
- An internal candidate with knowledge of the students and the community is best to direct the program.
- Synchronize schedules among schools to facilitate the program among various schools.
- Because this program is for high school juniors and seniors, there is a constant churn and cyclical nature to the work. The individual in charge of the program should be indefatigable.

NOTE

1. Jackel, Molly. "Wisdom of the (Multi) Ages: Students Learn by Teaching." Edutopia. June 8, 2008. http://www.edutopia.org/multiage-classroom-looping-peer-mentoring (accessed July 18, 2015).

Part V

Systems

Operational Support Systems Are Necessary as Well

Chapter Seventeen

Structure

Re-structuring often fails because of the focus on moving "boxes" and shifting reporting lines rather than addressing root causes.

—The Bridgespan Group [1]

Lack of progress is frustrating. Making incremental changes to your traditional pedagogy probably isn't going to dramatically improve the results. No matter the size or demographics of your district, if you intend to transform your organization to one with a long record of outstanding achievement and zero dropouts as a result, your organizational structure should encourage and support disruptive innovation.

In a student-centered environment like performance-based education, it is not only the classrooms that are flipped, but also the entire organizational hierarchy. If you were to do an "org chart," the students would be at the top!

Intent

Zero dropouts is one outcome of a version of performance-based education, but not a purpose. Of course, the only way to teach students is to keep them in school. Every child learns differently, and the purpose of the competency-based methodology and disruptive student-centered innovation is not just to keep everyone in school but to put each student into the environment where they learn best.

The purpose of your organization's hierarchical structure is to provide a barrier-free environment to accomplish this. If the reporting structure or the job assignments are preventing student success, then they should be changed. Success for a student in their life's work is the ultimate goal.

Innovation

Innovation comes in two varieties: disruptive and incremental. Incremental innovation creates new and improved ways of continuing existing practice. Disruptive innovation reinvents the status quo.

Even though performance-based learning may appear to be incremental innovation, it is actually disruptive. Educational institutions are historically risk averse. Disruptive innovation will take most districts and their leaders out of their comfort zones.

Some districts take the diplomatic approach and ignore innovation altogether. As if not recognizing innovation will make it less significant, or (even better) make it disappear.

Other districts create departments or cells within the educational organization that are responsible for innovating.

Whether it's the iZone in the New York City Department of Education or The Office of Innovation and Incubation in the Chicago Public Schools, these entities are supposed to encourage innovation from within by eliminating barriers, evaluating new products, and taking the pilot programs that work to scale.

Because the work of the innovation department is often fluid and undefined, many of these departments get organizational overload. The number of departments that report to them is often increased, and the innovation that was their original assignment can get bogged down by the volume of work among the everyday responsibilities for technology, student placement or Junior Reserve Officer Training Corps (JROTC).

Stephen Covey talks about paying attention to the responsibilities that are important, and not getting seduced by the everyday deadlines that are urgent.[2] As the organizational assignments build up, it is natural to handle the urgent and postpone the important. This is one of the reasons that a department of innovation and a position of "chief innovation officer" may be less effective than a more distributed model.

Arranging the Boxes

The work of creating an organizational structure for performance-based education is important, but also trivial. It is important because an appropriate structure should make the change in methodologies easier to accomplish. It signals that something important is happening. It is trivial because structure alone will not accomplish the conversion. A perfectly designed organizational structure will only serve to make a transition smoother, not create the change.

The Bridgespan Group has developed a presentation called Designing an Effective Organizational Structure. In that presentation, they divide the organizational structure into five distinct elements: leadership, decision making and structure, people, work processes and systems, and culture.[3] A redesigned organizational structure should take all of the five elements into account.

An organization built to innovate cannot exist solely on the creativity of the boss. Each level of leadership must understand the authority that is delegated to them. Intentional and unconditional delegation fosters the success of an organization focused upon disruptive innovation.

Other Examples

The literature about creative organizations like Apple and Google, or more conventional organizations that have set out to innovate like 3M or Procter and Gamble, describes organizational structures meant to foster creativity. Each has their own idea of what that structure should be.

Some organizations believe that a cooperative effort involving all employees makes more sense. This is the Bell Laboratories, Toyota, or early Google model. Others isolate their creatives. This is what Apple did with the Macintosh team and what Lockheed-Martin created with Skunkworks. Both models have generated innovative solutions.

Since the implementation of a version of performance-based learning should be a product of all of its educational professionals, the Toyota or Bell Labs model of organization will be more effective. In both large and small districts, the opportunity to create new ideas must be shared. The structure should be flat and the leadership distributed.

However, flatter is not necessarily better for everyone. In early 2015, online retailer Zappos decided to reorganize the company, flattening its hierarchy by eliminating managers and job titles. They offered a severance package to those employees who wanted to leave. The company reported a positive outcome since only 14 percent of their employees took the buyout, and they had anticipated that it would be more. The media reported the story as a negative outcome. What do you think?

Adjusting the Workload for Professional Development

Much of the lore of the effective teacher describes "the most effective" as a practitioner who does their work in isolation. In fact, the current literature on education reform is filled with tips on hiring and retaining the best, as if professional development does not exist. Or, at least, it is less important than identifying, hiring, and retaining those with "the right stuff."

Everyone should model learning in education. The culture is collaborative, professional, and student centered. A minimum of two hours per week of protected staff development time should be made available for certified staff during the school year by creating early-release days or using other means and methods. Frequent, collaborative, and targeted professional development creates effective teachers and increases social capital.

Classroom teachers and school administrators are overloaded with paperwork. Many question the productivity of so much documentation. In some cases, the judicious use of technology has helped; in others it has actually increased the burden.

Enlist staff support for something new by lightening the workload. Look for opportunities to eliminate or consolidate as much as possible. In his "Box of Less," Matthew May describes an exercise he calls Burn the Stupid Rule. He challenges the readers to list all of the rules in their organization that are excessive, confusing, wasteful, unnatural, hazardous, hard to use, or ugly. Then banish them forever.[4]

Lisa Bodell, in her book *Kill the Company*, suggests putting all the rules that get in the way of productivity in a matrix with "hard to easy to eliminate" on the vertical axis and the potential impact on productivity (low to high) on the horizontal. Why not eliminate those that are on the top right, which are easy to eliminate and have high impact on staff productivity? Bodell believes this is an opportunity for a quick win.[5]

May and Bodell suggest two ways of making more time available by eliminating time-consuming rules. Most of the rules in education involve documentation (i.e., paperwork). By eliminating the "busywork" and making professional development time available, you send several important signals—a growth mindset regarding your professional staff, the importance of lifelong learning, and the critical nature of the transition to performance-based learning.

Even the most nuanced structure will not create a single positive result. However, structure is a reflection of the district's values. Do not expect structure alone to solve issues. Work on a school's climate and culture, not the hierarchy, to make the real difference.

Leadership

A purposeful and coherent vision must come from the district team. Priorities and targets must be set, and everyone from members of the board, the superintendent, and the executive staff must have one message and one interpretation of what is important and what is to be accomplished. At one district, that meant that no child fails, no child is held back, and no child drops out. Your interpretation of putting every student into an environment where they will learn best may be somewhat different. The purpose remains the same.

Communication

The communication related to structure must contain no surprises. After much discussion and deliberation, a decision regarding organizational structure should be obvious. If it's not obvious, you haven't discussed it enough.

TregoEd has a great tool for decision making they call Decision Analysis. After stating the decision to be made, descriptions of the objectives are listed and weighted between 1 (the lowest) and 10 (the highest). The weights are then hidden, and the alternatives are listed and scored from 1 to 10 against each objective. The scores are multiplied by the weights to arrive at a total score for each objective and then totaled for each alternative. Once all the scores are totaled, the risks of selecting the highest scoring alternatives are evaluated and a selection is made.[6]

The beauty of this methodology is that if it is facilitated well, it documents and clarifies the logic behind the decision in an understandable and transparent fashion that surfaces all the issues that had an impact on the decision. It is a story that can be told and retold with fidelity.

Communication

The organizational structure should facilitate the sharing of information. Amy Lyman says there are three reasons for doing so: to promote understanding, to enhance participation, and to extend influence.[7]

Communication is not monologue. It is dialogue. If you are sharing information but not allowing response or feedback, you have not communicated. By doing so, you are conveying a lack of respect for the recipient and a lack of interest in what they might have to say. If you are changing the way you do business from traditional pedagogy to your version of performance-based learning, you need all the support you can get.

Support

To provide support for performance-based education and an organization built for creativity, the organizational structure must be nimble enough to act quickly upon suggestions and ideas from the field and thoughtful enough to consider the efficacy of those ideas. Once a decision is made to implement a suggestion, every effort is made to ensure its success.

This does not mean that every idea will be implemented intact as first suggested, but it does mean that every idea will be given serious consideration. And that most, if not all, will receive administrative encouragement and be given a fair trial.

Changing the overall educational construct is clearly the responsibility of district leadership, but ideas that have a smaller effect should be managed at the local level. This is particularly important for larger districts. The founders of Google originally decided that there were to be no managers, and it would have an egalitarian and flat organizational structure. They found that too many day-to-day decisions were ending up on their desk for a decision. It is not necessary for district leadership to decide everything. Responsibility should be distributed to the level most affected by the decision.

Structure will also support the performance-based concept by having improvements discussed and implemented at the professional learning community level. The teachers collaborate to improve their pedagogy or add to their repertoire.

Scope

While the hierarchy tends to be the focus when a district reorganizes, Bridgespan says that the location and ordering of "the boxes" in the organization chart is not as important as the links between the boxes. [8] School systems are often organized into silos by function with clear roles and responsibilities, but there should be cross-functional decision-making links as well. This strengthens and supports the common strategies and objectives. The inclusion of links to other functions also creates an awareness of related issues that would otherwise not be considered.

Strategy and Reach

Jeffrey Pfeffer and Robert Sutton have a chapter in their book, *The Knowing-Doing Gap*, in which they explain that institutional memory is often used as a substitute for thinking. "The organization's memory, embodied in precedents, customs of often unknown origin, stories about how things have always been and used to be, and standard operating procedures, becomes used as a substitute for taking wise action." [9]

It is important that the organizational structure allows leaders unconstrained access to individuals who do not substitute institutional memory for clear logic. Consider creating a small advisory group that cuts across all levels of the district hierarchy. Or select members of your leadership team specifically for this quality. Those that promote change must also be willing to change themselves.

Structural "reach" refers to the number of people a leader is able to effectively supervise. In June of 2015, New York City School's chancellor Carmen Farina's massive reorganization created borough field-support centers. The reach of each staff member in the help centers was roughly three schools each. [10]

Reach, in this case, does not refer to a day-to-day supervisory role but, rather, to a position of influence and assistance. Of course, it remains to be seen how Farina's will work, but the concept appears to be sound. The creation of a position of influence with a span of control of about three schools and four hundred staff members seems manageable and is typical of many organizations.

Most superintendents will reorganize within their first year and rarely change the reporting structure after that. It is interesting that this is contrary to the current trend in business, according to Gary L. Nielson and Julie Wulf. They say new CEOs tend to initially gather more direct reports (since they want to understand the scope of the business). Once they gain familiarity with the players, they frequently reduce their direct reports by as much as half.[11]

Create a more fluid structure that allows the superintendent to move positions in and out of a direct report as an indicator of the importance of the task assignments. For example, during a major redistricting effort, the superintendent may want the individual responsible for student assignment as a direct report. At the conclusion of that effort the structure could return to its former configuration.

Whether through lack of attention or conflict avoidance, legacy structures and remnants of previous decisions tend to be a pervasive condition of educational organizations. A staff member with deep knowledge of the organization and its processes should be given the task of cleaning these "cobwebs" from the past. A reorganizing directive that is clear about legacy operations is far more effective than one that leaves many loose ends to resolve.

Timing

Adjust the organizational chart over time. If there are barriers that are not optimizing the work flow, they should be eliminated. Have sufficient flexibility in position descriptions to allow for adjustments in responsibilities without changes to reporting structure.

The logistics of making a structural change might be daunting but are not necessarily as complex as they first appear. It is recommended that the changes in structure occur as one of the last, not the first, changes made. Although there are responsibilities and duties that are correlated to performance-based education, there is no single structure that is best in every circumstance.

Time is your friend in this case; as the work progresses the hierarchical needs will become clear and dictate the structure. Some of your veteran staff may receive additional duties and others may be appointed to other jobs. Some new people will be hired to fill newly created positions.

There should be no rush to judgment regarding structure. In New York City, Chancellor Farina held the position of deputy between 2004 and 2006 and was appointed chancellor in 2013. Although she was intimately familiar with the system, she waited two years before engineering this reorganization.

Continuum

Lack of consistency in actions and/or message will face criticism for a lack of authenticity. If a version of performance-based education is to be implemented in your district, then district leadership must "walk the talk" twenty-four hours a day. The organizational structure should reinforce that consistency. Alignment to the district's established principles is critical.

Staffing

Having the appropriate talent in the right positions is necessary to accomplish the objectives. While the content experts and experienced practitioners are admired and often promoted, it is those with the social competence and the ability to influence their colleagues that are more likely to get the work done. Those with enthusiasm for the vision of the district and empathy for the teachers, the students, the parents, and the community will be far more successful in the long term.

Assessment and Analysis

Objective data may not be helpful for evaluation or structure. Gather informal comments and subjective input to decide whether the arrangement is appropriate. If successful outcomes are being limited by the structure, the hierarchy should be changed.

Logistics

Any structural reorganization should be done with the input of reliable (i.e., not self-serving) incumbents. It should also provide clarity as to responsibilities and reporting structure. The communication about a reorganization must explain the purpose in detail so that the logic of the structural changes are immediately obvious. Everyone should know to whom they will report, what they are supposed to do, and why they are supposed to do it.

The ultimate question is this: If you had to start over from scratch and all the lines between the boxes on the org chart were erased, is this the way you would organize?

Mistakes

Ignoring the cross-functional links between assignments can be a problem. These links can be informal (dotted lines in the org chart). Formal links (hard lines in the org chart) as expressions of cross-functional relationships result in a matrix organization structure, and there are very few successful examples of that type of structure in the educational environment.

Some Points to Remember about Structure

- Adjust the structure last; get the right people first.
- Innovation comes in two forms: incremental and disruptive. Your organizational structure should foster and support disruptive innovation. As a collaborative effort within the district, disruptive innovation should be the responsibility of all, not just a specialized department.
- Leadership, decision making and structure, people, work processes and systems, and culture should all be considered when designing structure. [12]
- For best results, structure should be flat and leadership distributed.
- Structure alone will not solve issues.
- The ultimate purpose for the reorganization is student success in their life choices.
- Communication is not publicity or information sharing, but dialogue.
- Cross-functional connections within the structure help focus the organization on its priorities.
- The reach of one influential staff member needs to be around four hundred people within the district. This person serves as coach, advisor, and mentor as well as problem solver.
- A fluid structure is more productive. Loose ends and unresolved legacy issues are signs of a poor plan.
- Align structure to the organization's principles.
- The ultimate question is this: If you had to start over from scratch and erase all the lines between the boxes on the org chart, is this the way you would organize?

NOTES

1. The Bridgespan Group. "Designing an Effective Organization Structure." Presentation, Boston: The Bridgespan Group, 2009.
2. Covey, Stephen R. *The Seven Habits of Highly Effective People*. New York: Free Press, 1989.
3. The Bridgespan Group, "Designing an Effective Organization Structure.
4. May, Matthew. "Box of Less." Mathewemay.com. 2012. http://matthewemay. matthewemay.netdna-cdn.com/wp-content/uploads/2012/11/Box-of-Less.pdf (accessed September 2, 2015).
5. Bodell, Lisa. *Kill the Company*. Brookline: Bibliomotion, 2012.
6. Richetti, Cynthia, and Benjamin Tregoe. *Analytic Processes for School Leaders*. Alexandria, VA: Association for Supervision and Curriculum Development, 2001.
7. Lyman, Amy. *The Trustworthy Leader*. San Francisco: Jossey-Bass, 2012.
8. The Bridgespan Group, "Designing an Effective Organization Structure."
9. Pfeffer, Jeffrey, and Robert I. Sutton. *The Knowing-Doing Gap*. Cambridge, MA: Harvard Business School Press, 2000.
10. Wall, Patrick. "City Launches School-Support Centers, a Key Element of Farina's System Shakeup." Chalkbeat. July 1, 2015. http://ny.chalkbeat.org/2015/07/01/city-launches-support-centers-a-key-element-of-farina's-system-shakeup/#.VZSWB_n9mUI (accessed July 2, 2015).

11. Nielson, Gary L., and Julie Wulf. "How Many Direct Reports?" *Harvard Business Review* 90(4), 2012.

12. The Bridgespan Group, Designing an Effective Organization Structure.

Chapter Eighteen

Technology

Science and technology revolutionize our lives, but memory, tradition and myth frame our response.

—Arthur Schlesinger

Although some organizations acquire tools as a status symbol, most acquire tools because of what they allow us to do. There are some tools that are hard to imagine doing without in a modern society, and technology is one of those. And while technology in education has been introduced with less than consistent results, it is still hard to imagine modern education without any of the tools of technology.

Technology has put the world of information into the hands of students. For better or worse, this has changed education forever. Teachers who have incorporated technology into their classrooms say that pedagogy has become more student centered, and their program delivery has become more facilitating and coaching, and less knowledge delivery. Students are no longer just knowledge consumers, they are active discoverers.

Purpose

There are many reasons to integrate technology into your classrooms, from the need to keep reference material current to the need to model digital citizenship to your students. These tools can make class content more relevant and more engaging for students.

Technology can also be used as a tool to help teachers collect and analyze data about student progress. As teachers are delegated more responsibilities, it is important to lighten the load wherever possible. Technology can help to do that, but it generally takes some professional development in order to accomplish the end result.

Decisions

Glenn Meeks correctly points out in *Creating a Culture of Learning* that if you are going to introduce technology into your classrooms and schools, you must first decide what you want to accomplish. Then select which tools to use. It is less about the tools and more about the purpose.[1]

After being involved in a few massive technology introduction projects and finding that many of the faculty were not using the tools to their potential, Meeks decided that a better process was required. The usual reaction to lack of use is more training for the teachers, but he sees it as a much bigger issue than that.

The introduction of technology requires the support and interaction of all seven of the silos that Meeks identifies: infrastructure, facilities, professional development, policies/procedures, technical support, systems/loose equipment, and what/how kids learn. If you don't include all seven in your implementation plans and get others' cooperation, you have set yourself up for failure.

Placement

The use of technology has improved our ability to identify student progress or lack thereof. Data in its most usable forms allows teachers to see where students are struggling and provide assistance. Data can also show teachers the students that have mastered the content and need further challenges.

In order to be useful, the data must be easy to access and the reports simple to analyze. The interpretations belong to the educators, but the creation of a report, either for an entire class or for an individual student, cannot be overly complex.

Data gathered is clearly useful for all sorts of analyses. It is also useful in preparing a personalized individual education plan for each student. The carryover of this material, which contains teacher observations and student comments as well as facts and figures, helps personalize learning for each child. This is especially important in accelerated-learning delivery since it would be easy to lose track of a specific student's efforts and progress because they may be assigned to various grade-level content areas.

Collaboration

Technology doesn't just give us better or faster tools and access to data, it has actually changed the way we work and learn.

Victoria Bergsagel, CEO of Architects of Achievement, believes that technology used thoughtfully can enhance the learning environment. "Students today prefer active learning, in welcoming spaces, with people who take an interest in them and their curiosities. Technology, when used appropriately, can significantly enhance such collaboration."[2]

Peer-to-peer learning and cross-age mentoring are made possible through the use of electronic devices. Professional learning communities stay in touch through the use of e-mail and text messaging as well as their face-to-face meetings.

Classroom Amplification

One simple and relatively inexpensive technology is the amplification of a teacher's voice in the classroom. Classroom amplification systems include loudspeakers (typically mounted on the walls or in the ceiling), a receiver/ amplifier, and a wireless microphone that transmits the teacher's voice throughout the room.

This was originally used for the students in a hearing-impaired classroom, but classroom amplification has also been shown to improve outcomes with students who can hear within the normal range. Why?

If the teacher is speaking to the class at normal volume at the front of the classroom, the only students who can distinctly hear every word are 75 percent of those in the first three rows. The MARRS study by the U.S. Department of Education found that 20–25 percent or more of the current school population has academic difficulties coexisting with minimal hearing loss (defined as 15–40 dB).[3] So about 25 percent of those in the first three rows have missed some of what is said.

Distance also affects speech intelligibility. Some teachers compensate for this by either raising their voice or by traveling through the classroom as they present the lesson, but neither is as good a solution as classroom amplification.

The sound quality of intelligible speech degrades at normal volume at a distance of ten to twelve feet. High-frequency speech (76 percent of teachers are women) tends to degrade even faster. So in a classroom without voice amplification, only a fraction of the content is being delivered. No wonder classroom amplification increases academic outcomes.

Gaming

The use of gaming and the associated skills are increasingly being used as learning tools. Some have speculated that the design and production of electronic games may be one of the twenty-first-century careers for which we will need to prepare our students.

Games can not only be used as powerful learning tools but also as therapy. Some scientists believe that by playing the game Project Evo, you can improve a range of cognitive skills and, by extension, relieve a range of symptoms related to cognitive disorders like ADHD, depression, and autism.[4]

Equity

Access to technology is one of the most challenging aspects of technology in education. There is not one best practice for providing equitable access, but some districts have developed some creative solutions.

Subsidized lease rates, allowing students use of a device while in school, and "bring-your-own-device" programs have all been used to get personal devices into the hands of every child. But equity of distribution is only part of the problem.

High-poverty students often have no access to reliable or high-speed Internet service at home, and many innovations (e.g., flipped classrooms) require students to use the Internet before and after school. One option could be Wi-Fi on buses. Some Internet service providers offer connections for home and school as part of their service package. When no service is available, sending the lessons home on a disc or thumb drive may be the answer.

Leaders

Like almost everything else, leadership that models technology integration and expertise is a powerful motivator. Most superintendents didn't begin using computers and e-mail until about 2005. Previous to that, dictation was used for correspondence and the telephone for personal communication. Superintendents that are early adopters are still a small minority.

Current demographics would suggest that the majority of district staff members are probably not digital natives, either. This means that comfort and proficiency with technology comes as result of practice and professional development. Even digital natives should not attempt technology integration solo. District leadership will succeed in this field by relying upon the expertise of a group of trusted advisors.

The International Society for Technology in Education has said there are fourteen essential conditions necessary to effectively leverage technology for learning. They also offer a free Lead and Transform Diagnostic Tool on their website to plan and analyze a district's path to technology integration. These are the essential conditions:

1. Developing a shared vision for educational technology among all education stakeholders;

2. Empowering stakeholders at every level to be leaders in effecting change;

3. Following a systematic plan aligned with a shared vision for school effectiveness and student learning through the infusion of information and communication technology (ICT) and digital learning resources;

4. Supporting technology infrastructure, personnel, digital resources, and staff development with consistent and ongoing funding;

5. Giving all students, teachers, staff, and school leaders robust and reliable connectivity and access to current and emerging technologies and digital resources;

6. Staffing with educators, support personnel, and others skilled in the selection and effective use of appropriate ICT resources;

7. Providing educators with access to technology-related professional learning plans and opportunities as well as dedicated time to practice and share ideas;

8. Giving educators and students access to reliable assistance for maintaining, renewing, and using ICT and digital learning resources;

9. Creating content standards and related digital curriculum resources that align with and support digital-age learning and work;

10. Developing a continuum of planning, teaching, and assessment, all centered on the needs and abilities of the students;

11. Continuously assessing and evaluating teaching, learning, leadership, and the use of ICT and digital resources;

12. Connecting leaders and educators to maintain partnerships and collaboration within the community to support and fund the use of ICT and digital learning resources;

13. Supporting the use of ICT and other digital resources through policies, financial plans, accountability measures, and incentive structures for both learning and district/school operations; and

14. Developing policies and initiatives at the national, regional, and local levels to support schools and teacher preparation programs in the effective implementation of technology for achieving curriculum and learning technology (ICT) standards.[5]

Larger districts will likely find it more challenging to assure equity. The magnitude of the exercises, purchase, distribution, and training on the electronic devices will probably need to be phased in, and those in the first phase should be updated and in sync with those in the final phase. Don't forget funding for the refresh of hardware and software. An industry rule of thumb is that downtime can be minimized by having an additional 4 percent to 10 percent of "attic stock" of hardware for those that break and need repair.

Communication

The inclusion of technology into the educational delivery process has more or less ceased to be controversial. The use of these tools that we use in our everyday lives to improve education seems almost routine at this point.

The messaging around a one-to-one device initiative or a bring-your-own-device program must be closely tied to equity of access. Before a new technology program is rolled out, the communication around how everyone can enjoy access to these tools must be carefully constructed. Home Internet access is still not ubiquitous, even in urban areas. Every effort should be made to get access for all students. Otherwise, the use of technology becomes another differentiator between the haves and the have nots. Some districts have created programs with alternative methods of obtaining devices and additional Wi-Fi access attempts to mediate this.

Support

Local businesses, both large and small, understand the value and the need for students to be computer literate. They can be a source of support for technology initiatives. The ability of the school system to offer a tax write-off is sometimes an incentive as well. Unfortunately, this is sometimes used by businesses as a way to donate out-of-date equipment. So care must be taken to accept only donations that will be of use to the academic program. Consider using an online auction site to sell donated surplus technology.

Parent-teacher associations are another source of support for technology initiatives. Their ability to fund-raise around a specific goal is often remarkable. Again, care must be taken to make sure the donations are complementary to the existing equipment and program.

Scope

You must begin by working with what you have available. Kristen Weller describes in a short video how she uses one iPad in her math classroom at P. K. Yonge Developmental Research School in Gainesville, Florida.[6]

Plan the introduction of technology into your academic program carefully. Glenn Meeks writes, "Creating a twenty-first century student-centered learning environment for all instructional spaces in an entire district is a very complex process involving many elements."[7]

Many school districts are required to submit a technology plan to the state educational agency for review. Fulfilling this requirement is a good place to begin thinking about how technology will be integrated into your instructional program delivery.

Strategy and Reach

Technology integration is not always a good thing. Amazon recently introduced the dash button, a way to order what you need, when you need it. Mark Wilson reviewed it for *Fast Company* and was very disappointed. Although the idea of having a button on your washing machine that you can push whenever you need more detergent seems to be convenient, apparently the choices and pricing are limited and the delivery time of forty-eight hours is not always convenient.[8]

Unfamiliar with what might be available? Tap outside and in-house expertise, or both. Technology changes so fast that it is difficult for one person to be aware of everything that is available. Trust, but verify sources.

The reach for technology integration must be both district-wide and yet personal. Look at voice enhancement as an example. Some districts will install audio reinforcement at every teaching station, although some teachers will never use it. Others do not install it in any classroom. Neither is the best solution. The environment you create for technology integration should be flexible enough to get the tools to those teachers who want them but targeted enough to provide the right tools to every teacher to enhance their program delivery.

You must maintain a delicate balance between mass distribution and targeted distribution. Every teacher may not use every piece of software or voice enhancement available. The need for specialized software or hardware should be determined by the individual teacher and the technology-integration specialists.

Steve Jobs famously discounted focus group research, referring to the Henry Ford quote about not asking his customers what they wanted because they would have said a faster horse.[9] Some of the same may be true for educators. So the strategy must be both inward looking and outward facing: How do we fix this problem (internal), or what would Steve Jobs do (external)?

Timing

Announcing an expensive technology integration program is not the best thing to do just before a vote on a controversial bond referendum, but announcing that the next bond referendum will include an expensive technology integration program to provide every student with current technology might work out just fine.

Using the fiscal year's fund balance to pay for the first phase of a program could be acceptable, as long as the fund balance isn't so large that it negatively impacts the concurrent budget request. An increase in the millage rate for technology is often well received, but not if there has just been an exposé in the local paper about wasteful spending in the district.

Much of this is common sense. The current teacher shortages are attributed to the stagnant wages in many states. It's not a good idea for the district to buy everyone a new electronic device if the teachers have just been told that once again they will not get a raise.

Continuum

Getting the technology in place is only the first step in a continuous process. Don't forget the professional development in the use of the new tools, the technical support for the inevitable glitches, and adequate facility accommodations for the equipment (including air-conditioning and power), and plan for the cost of the refresh program (the rule of thumb is to refresh every three years).

Staffing

This is a very subjective aspect of technology. It is not strictly generational (both Bill Gates and Steve Jobs were baby boomers born in 1955), nor is it based entirely on expertise (either technical or educational). The two characteristics that seem most prevalent in those that adapt to and adopt technology are an innate curiosity coupled with a lack of intimidation by new things. The questions you use to vet a candidate should identify these qualities, particularly when hiring for your technical positions.

Assessment and Analysis

Technology in all its forms is a tool. If the tool isn't helping with the task, it comes down to a lack of skill or use of the wrong tool. Your questions in this case are about comfort and expertise. You should keep Jellison's J-curve in mind (i.e., do not expect immediate improvement). In fact, initial results will be worse than what has been the norm, but that will not be the ultimate trajectory.

Jellison has an interesting way of estimating the length of time it will take to change the outcome trajectory in a positive direction. Estimate the worst case. Now be optimistic and estimate best case. For the most realistic estimate of the time frame, split the difference. [10]

There are software packages available that will tell you exactly how much each teacher is using their technology. Like many other issues, the volume or quantity of usage doesn't always translate to the quality of use. One week, a teacher may use technology sparingly because there needs to be significant face-to-face discussion around a lesson. Another week, a teacher may use technology exclusively. You want each teacher to be comfortable and skillful in using the tools. Beyond that, precisely measuring actual usage is not productive.

Logistics

Professional development and technical support are the keys to ubiquitous technology usage. The best professional development is not done en masse, but by personal referral. Regardless, there are some technology skills that may be best conveyed to a group (e.g., grading and attendance) but others that can be done by referral. This could be as simple as, "Before we leave today I would like you to e-mail three of your colleagues that would benefit most from what we talked about today and invite them to our next session."

Security is always a concern with the introduction of technology. Lost or stolen flash drives have been the source of many security breaches lately. Bill Brown, CIO for Greenville (South Carolina) Schools has incorporated a simple system for retrieving data from lost flash drives. He has the district name and address printed on all the USB flash drives the district issues. (These are the only flash drives permitted to be used in the district's equipment.) When they are dropped in the parking lot or lost at the mall, as many as 80 percent of them are returned.

Mistakes

When you are trying to do something new, sometimes it doesn't work well or the way you anticipated. This happened repeatedly to the Wright brothers as they developed their flying machine at Kill Devil Hills in North Carolina. Wilbur, in his letters home, would often call these occurrences being "Jonah'd," referring to the character in the Bible.[11] Whether your work is as groundbreaking as theirs, or as mundane as making sure that the students and teachers in the temporary classrooms have access to the Internet, failure is going to be part of the process. The mistake is to give up when you are Jonah'd.

Technology in and of itself will not improve the delivery of academic programming. Like structure, technology is a tool that can provide certain benefits, but it must be used appropriately to derive those benefits. The simple presence of the tool will not accomplish much. It must be paired with and employed by a knowledgeable practitioner to accomplish a successful change in program delivery. When that happens, the connection of the student to the content can be incredible. When that doesn't happen, it is like the content and the student are on two different planets.

Some Points to Remember about Technology

- Technology is neither an innovation nor a status symbol. It is a tool. It is useful only if you know how you want to use it and what you want to accomplish.

- Your technology budget should include the tools, the technical support, the professional development, the attic stock, and the refresh.
- Include infrastructure, facilities, professional development, policies/procedures, technical support, systems/loose equipment, and what/how kids learn in your technology integration and implementation plans.
- Equity of access both at school and at home is one of the challenges of technology introduction. It can and has been solved by many districts in many different ways, but it must be addressed in the implementation plan.
- Leaders that model technology expertise are a powerful motivator.
- Monetize and maximize the potential of community connections for acquiring technology once you decide what will serve your purposes.
- Use whatever technology is available initially. If that means students share a device in the classroom, plan how to make it work. Scaling up to the district level requires careful planning. Most states require a technology plan. Use this as an opportunity.
- Utilize outside and in-house expertise for evaluation of hardware and software. Just as with medical issues, a second opinion is a good idea.
- Time the introduction of technology carefully. Since it is a significant expenditure, it usually draws attention. That attention can be negative if not timed appropriately.
- Hire for innate curiosity and lack of intimidation for trying new things.
- Usage alone is not the only indicator that technology is being used correctly for program delivery. Targeted professional development and technical support are the keys to widespread technology usage.
- Individual teachers should be given a voice in what is to be installed in their classrooms.

NOTES

1. Meeks, Glenn. *Creating a Culture of Learning.* Lanham, MD: Rowman & Littlefield, 2014.

2. Bergsagel, Victoria, e-mail to Michael K. Raible. CEO of Architects of Achievement (November 2, 2015).

3. U.S. Department of Education. "Mainstream Application Resource Room Study." The Institute for Enhanced Classroom Hearing. n.d. http://www.classroomhearing.org/research/marrsStudy.html (accessed November 20, 2015).

4. Dembosky, April. "'Play This Video Game and Call Me in the Morning.'" National Public Radio. August, 17, 2015. http://www.npr.org/sections/health-shots/2015/08/17/432004332/play-this-video-game-and-call-me-in-the-morning (accessed September 6, 2015).

5. "Essential Conditions." International Society for Technology in Education. 2015. http://www.iste.org/standards/essential-conditions (accessed July 14, 2015).

6. Weller, Kristen. "Blended Learning: Working with One iPad." Edutopia. November 12, 2014. http://www.edutopia.org/blog/blended-learning-working-one-ipad (accessed July 14, 2015).

7. Meeks, Glenn. *Creating a Culture of Learning.* Lanham, MD: Rowman & Littlefield, 2014.

8. Wilson, Mark. "Life with the Dash Button: Good Design for Amazon, Bad Design for Everyone Else." Fast Company. August 19, 2015. http://www.fastcodesign.com/3050044/life-with-the-dash-button-good-design-for-amazon-bad-design-for-everyone-else? (accessed August 19, 2015).

9. Isaacson, Walter. *Steve Jobs*. New York: Simon & Schuster, 2011

10. Jellison, Jerald. *Managing the Dynamics of Change*. New York: McGraw-Hill, 2006.

11. Howard, Fred. *Wilbur and Orville*. New York: Ballantine Books, 1987.

Chapter Nineteen

Resources and Budgeting

Native Americans have many sayings, and one of the wisest is this: "When you're riding a dead horse, the best strategy is to dismount." You don't change riders. You don't reorganize the herd. You don't put together a blue-ribbon commission of veterinarians. And you don't spend more money on feed. You get off and find yourself a new horse.

—David Osborne and Peter Hutchinson[1]

Public education organizations almost never generate revenue. Always being a supplicant agency has its drawbacks. Whether in a public or private funding agency, decision makers complain about education always begging for more money. So it is not surprising that schools and districts considering a transition to proficiency-based methods would decide not to do so because they feel they cannot afford it.

Regardless of the method of program delivery, maximizing the use of existing revenue sources is the first order of business in moving as much funding as possible to district priorities. Reviewing every aspect of the business to find savings and/or efficiencies should be part of the annual budgeting exercise.

Intent

The intent of this exercise is to be able to move as much funding as possible to your priorities. Every time money is saved in a category, it should be celebrated by saying, "Do you know how many (fill in the blank) we can buy with that?"

Expenditures

There are two basic categories of expenditures—operating and capital. The operating funds are used for day-to-day expenses. Everything from salaries to utility costs is paid with operating funds. Capital funds are used for major onetime expenses. The general rule of thumb is that capital improvements should last twenty years or more.

The school district's annual budget usually deals with operating funds. The capital budget is often funded through separate funding vehicles such as voter-approved general obligation bonds that require voter approval, or certificates of participation, which do not require voter approval.

There is no bright line that separates the two kinds of expenditures. Some operating expenses closely relate to capital projects, such as the cost of program management. These are sometimes funded through the capital budget and surplus operating funds are sometimes used for capital improvements (this is called pay-as-you-go or paygo).

Public/private partnerships, sale/leaseback arrangements, and capital leasing have been used in some districts to creatively finance capital improvements when traditional methods are not available. These have not been used widely, even though businesses that find themselves in similar circumstances (significant nonliquid real estate assets) frequently lease rather than own their facilities.

The limitations of bonded indebtedness have also constrained capital improvements for some districts in fast-growing areas from keeping up with the need for building additional capacity and for renovating existing facility inventory. Mobile classrooms are often used to solve for needed capacity. Unfortunately, since old buildings do not come with an expiration date, many districts are forced to continue to use outdated facilities that have long ago exceeded their useable lifespan.

Lack of capital-improvement funds forces schools and districts into making operational decisions that they would otherwise not make. A district in Virginia had so much additional capacity in their older buildings that when roofs began to fail, they simply moved into classrooms in another wing of the building and closed the classroom wing with the leaky roof.

The Theory of Constraints

Elizabeth Doty explains in an article in *Strategy + Business* that the theory of constraints governs progress in change initiatives. The theory of constraints is the idea that maximizing the activity of each part in a system actually reduces the output of the system. [2]

Budget deliberations can also be subjected to the theory of constraints. Instead of concentrating additional resources on all of the parts of the operating process, provide better resources to the part of the organization that is holding the rest of the system back by underperforming.

Doty describes the example of a scout troop on a hike used by Eliyahu Goldratt and Jeff Cox in *The Goal*.[3] The pace of the hike is set by the slowest scout, Herbie. The only way to improve the pace of the troop is to get Herbie to hike faster. Anything else done is extraneous.

Knowing this, if you want the troop to hike faster, you lighten Herbie's load, make sure he is comfortable, give him any equipment he might need to hike faster, and make him the line leader to set the pace.

Find your "Herbie." What is controlling the pace of accomplishing your goals? Applying resources to the task or department that is constraining progress may be the key to making substantial progress on your goals. This is the reason for the redistribution of resources in the annual budget process.

Alignment

Of course, you must first decide what your key goals are and their relative priority. By doing so, you have now created a means by which to measure the application of resources (not just funding, but staffing as well). Stephen Covey refers to this as a "direct line of sight."[4]

For example, there are two initiatives in the energy manager's latest proposed budget. The first involves an investment in software that will turn the power off on all of the computers in the schools at times that can be specified from a central location and can be specific to a school, a group of computers, or each individual device. Other districts that have done this have averaged savings of 5 percent on their electric bills.

In the other initiative, students participate in an energy-savings program in which they monitor and attempt to reduce energy consumption within their school. This program requires the installation of energy-monitoring devices throughout a participating school and the creation of an energy "dashboard," accessible to the students, that shows real-time usage of all utilities.

The first cost and ongoing licensing fees are about the same for both proposed initiatives. The savings are also about the same. Assume you have the funds to begin one of the programs. How do you decide which one to authorize?

Resources need to be applied to leverage the goals of the district. As difficult as it is, this decision must be made on an annual basis for every program in the system. The legacy programs are the hardest ones to analyze because they not only have incumbent staff, but implied expectations.

Why are we here? What do we want to accomplish? How will this program increase our progress toward that goal? The TregoEd decision-making protocols[5] can be applied in these circumstances very easily. This methodology not only helps identify the important characteristics of each process but allows you to quickly assign weights to each.

As Stephen Covey reminds us in *The 8th Habit*, the organizational goals should be well defined and small in number.[6] There should be a direct line of sight between the tasks proposed for funding and what is to be accomplished. These are not the targets listed in a twenty-page balanced scorecard, but the two or three goals that summarize the purpose of the district.

Leaders

A financial leadership team that focuses solely on compliance will not be successful at optimizing resources. In order to be successful, the superintendent and the school district's financial officer must work as a team to develop innovative ways to maximize the district's traditional funding and find new sources of revenue. They must be fully aware of the limitations that are placed upon the resources and work to maximize the leverage of those funds. They must be creative and entrepreneurial because the resources are scarce. Supplemental sources of revenue must be explored, cultivated, and developed.

Not that compliance should be given short shrift. Because of issues of local politics, district leadership may sometimes be tempted to circumvent the will of their board by simply not asking about a specific decision.

In 2014, the St. Joseph (Missouri) School District received a rebate from their insurance company. The superintendent decided to distribute that money in $5,000 stipends to some of his deserving administrators. Problem is, he neglected to inform his board. As of April 10, 2014, the state auditor, the U.S. Department of Education, and the Federal Bureau of Investigation were investigating.[7]

Much of the literature about schools and money delves deeply into the financial regulations and mechanisms or the economics of education. Clearly, improving operating efficiencies and saving money in the process permits a district to plow more funding into instruction.

However, other considerations must also be factored in. If, for example, state education regulations permitted local jurisdictions to decide whether or not to provide transportation for students, and in order to save money the district decided to forego transportation to its schools, the results may well be devastating for segments of the school population. Those savings in funds would probably not be good for education.

So one of the keys to effective resource allocation is analyzing the downstream effects of possible expenditures or savings and prioritizing them accordingly. Look at effect size and its correlation to the district's strategic plan to optimize your priorities. Many districts use site-based budgeting to push the decisions for the budget priorities into the hands of the administrators that actually make the expenditures.

The dilemma with site-based budgeting is in arriving at a fair distribution of funds for each site. There is usually not a reward for returning unexpended funds. So that means sites that have been allocated more than they need can purchase excess items or services, while those that have not been given enough struggle to balance needs and available funds.

Creativity and resource allocation can be mutually exclusive topics in public education, but district leaders who know and understand the rules see those rules as constraints, not necessarily limitations. Matthew May's fourth law of subtraction is that creativity thrives under intelligent constraints.[8] How can you monetize existing resources? How can you create profit centers? What other funding is available from local businesses or grant-funding organizations?

Communication

Finding your voice on this aspect of performance-based education must be nuanced. It is dependent upon the attitude of the community and the popularity of the district leadership. Too much solicitation begins to sound like a pledge drive for the local public radio station; too little and you leave funding on the table. Be sensitive to the windows of opportunity for support.

Charlotte-Mecklenburg Schools (CMS) in North Carolina identified the schools in the district that were in the greatest need of resources and began a conversation with community benefactors and corporations about leveraging their contributions exclusively on those nine schools for a period of five years. Ultimately, $55 million was pledged by the donors, and a public/ private partnership was formed to ensure progress was made. CMS has been required to submit a report annually on the results of their grant.[9]

The grant funding will come with strings. Those in business are used to getting a return on investment. Philanthropic organizations, such as the Gates Foundation, will require documentation of expected results in grant applications and request a report demonstrating the effect of the expenditure when the grant is ended.

Communication to the elected decision makers and to the constituents in the community regarding budgets and expenditures is necessary for transparency and support. In many cases, it is required by law. Seek to communicate beyond compliance. Use the reporting opportunity to demonstrate how a judicious use of the resources provided has given the students in the community advantages that others do not have.

Support

As a public school district, you must rely on the support of your community (elected officials, individuals, and businesses) for just about everything, but especially funding. With the conversion to a performance-based education platform, that support is even more critical to success. A district in which the community withholds their support is simply not going to survive, regardless of the value of the educational platform.

Securing support is not just about the asking during the budget cycle. It must be done with frequent transparent communication throughout the year. Decisions on funding a budget increase are made long before the annual budget request.

Scope

While the broad support of the community is a strong asset, fund-raising requires tangible targets. Whether it is the fifth graders trip to Washington, DC, or the corporate sponsorship of the football stadium, there needs to be a tangible result. The rule of thumb is this: the bigger the request, the better the chances that someone will want to hang a plaque on it.

Strategy and Reach

Effective use of resources is the strategy. Optimize your existing funding. Target your fund-raising to specific improvements. Monetize your assets. Transparency is paramount. Be sensitive to any indication of public distrust, and address it immediately because it will affect your fund-raising. This effort should be coordinated and documented. There is nothing worse than two people asking the same individual or company for a contribution for the same purpose.

Again, gratitude should be heartfelt and genuine, and personal notes are in order here. The message is that you understand that donors have a choice as to where they spend their money and that you appreciate their faith in the school system.

Timing

If a district's revenue source is the state, and the annual budget is dependent upon legislative action and not millage, there is usually a problem with sequence. If the legislature does not finish its work in June, it puts tremendous pressure on the district hiring process. The largest pool of staff is available in May and June. If a district is unable to hire until August because they do not know what positions will be authorized by the state, they are forced to pick from a much smaller pool of available employees. And if legislative action is further delayed, the hiring pool is further depleted, and the situation further exacerbated.

Politics are politics, and it is sometimes difficult to get legislative bodies to agree to do something, even when they agree it needs to be done. Nonetheless, it is recommended that if the legislature is truly concerned about the quality of the schools they fund, they should consider making the decisions that affect the district hiring processes no later than June.

Continuum

The annual budgeting process often creates surpluses, sometimes as much as 2 percent of the total budget at the end of the fiscal year. Administrators in some cases wait until the end of the fiscal year to make onetime purchases of equipment or services that could be characterized as "nice-to-have," rather than "have-to-have." The same condition often occurs at the district level. A fund balance or surplus is developed during the fiscal year and is then expended in a flurry of last minute purchases.

Use these funds to further strategic goals, not for "Christmas in July." Prioritization of these expenditures should occur at the district level. Volume of purchasing should be monitored and budget administrators that have higher than average levels of purchasing toward the end of the fiscal year should be asked to explain the cause. The unintended consequence of an annual budget process is a "use it or lose it" mentality. And that will prevail, if not monitored and questioned.

Staffing

Accounting and budgeting are not disciplines that produce many innovative practitioners. If you find one, they are worth their weight in gold. If you need to train one, you must appeal to their fascination with puzzles and problem solving (the missing twenty-five cents on a balance sheet drives them crazy). The problem solvers at IDEO begin their sessions with a "How might we . . ." statement of the problem.[10] This may be a little too open-ended for the accountants, but keep working with them. Eventually they will understand that you do not want to break the rules, just solve a problem.

Assessment and Analysis

Both Educational Resource Strategies[11] and Rob Sanderson at Bank of America[12] use regression analysis and Pareto charts to analyze the data related to resources. These experts use these tools because they have a strong visual component. When the charts are assembled using the appropriate variables, it is easy to identify the outliers, those areas that may require attention.

This is also an area where a fresh perspective is useful. Bring in a supporter from the community with a financial background and no personal agenda to review the numbers with you. Some of the questions they raise may be naïve. Others may surface issues that had not been considered.

Logistics

Real estate agents will tell you that the quality of the school affects the value of residential property. Higher value real estate generates more taxes. And yet very few districts have been able to improve a school by monetizing that connection. This is not a theoretical argument, but one that needs to be made with hard data.

Budgeting is about making the most of your available resources—people, time, and money. "While the field of education already has a strong research base around the practices and characteristics of excellent schools, there has been less clarity around effective resources use."[13]

In their book *The Strategic School*, Karen Hawley Miles and Stephan Frank identify the practices and policies that thwart effective resource use. These are the issues that you must work to control if you are to use your resources to their best advantage:

- Lack of control over hiring and assignment;
- Limited available flexible teachers;
- Fragmented district professional development that doesn't match school needs;
- Contracts that restrict the use of teacher time;
- Limited support for new teachers;
- Funding mechanisms that average teacher costs instead of using actuals limiting available resources for schools with a majority of novice teachers;
- Career structures that reward longevity, not expertise;
- Assessments that don't provide timely or actionable information;
- Mandated class sizes;
- Limitations on interdisciplinary instruction and flexible grouping;
- Contractual limitations on the way time can be structured;
- Short student and teacher work days; and
- Rigid grade structures and course requirements.[14]

While a few of these items are clearly out of local control, many can be leveraged to create more effective use of resources.

Mistakes

This is work that must be done by professionals who understand the legal and accounting conventions. Lack of knowledge about legal provisions or ways that expenditures must be recorded will undoubtedly lead to trouble. Develop a close working relationship with your financial team. When in doubt, seek advice or assistance from a local professional.

Because we tend to be passionate about the programs we are requesting in the annual budget, it is easy to begin to take the budget process personally. Most budget decisions are not personal, but a matter of a funding authority doing their best to balance needs and revenue.

Some Points to Remember about Budgeting and Resources

- To maximize resources, annually review every aspect of the organization's operation to identify savings and efficiencies.
- Operating budgets pay for ongoing expenses (e.g., salaries). Capital budgets are used for major onetime expenditures (e.g., facilities).
- The theory of constraints can be used to apply additional resources. Align budget line items to accomplishing key goals. Find your "Herbie."
- Use *TregoEd* processes or similar methodologies to objectively prioritize funding.
- Compliance with regulations is only one aspect of financial management.
- Be sensitive to funding opportunities within the community.
- To the extent possible, seek appropriate budget timing that allows the district to hire in the best time frame (i.e., June budget finalized).
- Direct fund balance to accomplish goals. Make decisions centrally.
- Find financial managers that are problem solvers.
- Get budget advice from the community.

NOTES

1. Osborne, David, and Peter Hutchinson. *The Price of Government*. New York: Basic Books, 2004.

2. Doty, Elizabeth. "Finding the 'Herbie' in Your Change Initiative," *Strategy + Business*, Oct. 13, 2015. http://www.strategy-business.com/blog/Finding-the-Herbie-in-Your-Change-Initiative?gko=908bd.

3. Goldratt, Eliyahu, and Jeff Cox. *The Goal*. Great Barrington, MA: North River Press, 1986.

4. Covey, Stephen R. *The 8th Habit*. New York: Free Press, 2004.

5. "Description of Strategies." TregoEd. 2014. http://tregoed.org/strategies/description-of-strategies.html (accessed November 15, 2015).

6. Covey, *The 8th Habit*.

7. Zeff, Sam. "Stipend Scandal Erupts in St. Joseph Missouri." Ballotpedia. June 30, 2014. http://ballotpedia.org/Stipend_scandal_erupts_in_St._Joseph,_Missouri (accessed July 13, 2015).

8. May, Matthew E. *The Laws of Subtraction*. New York: McGraw-Hill, 2013.

9. Helms, Ann Doss. "Project LIFT First-Year Report: Lots of Work Remains." *Charlotte Observer*, March 27, 2014.

10. IDEO. "Design Thinking for Educators." d.school, The Hasso-Plattner Institute of Design at Stanford. 2012. http://www.designthinkingforeducators.com/ (accessed July 7, 2015).

11. Educational Resource Strategies. 2015. http://www.erstrategies.org/ (accessed August 3, 2015).

12. Sanderson, Rob, interview by Michael Raible. Vice president/operation project consultant, Bank of America (July 9, 2015).

13. Miles, Karen Hawley, and Stephen Frank. *The Strategic School*. Thousand Oaks, CA: Corwin Press, 2008.

14. Miles and Frank, *The Strategic School*.

Conclusion

Implementation

If you really want to do something, you'll find a way. If you don't, you'll find an excuse.

—Anonymous

Education should offer opportunities—the opportunity for every student to earn a high school diploma, the opportunity for every student to earn the credentials that translate to a living wage, and the opportunity for every student to succeed. Traditional education methods, despite many incremental innovations, have not fulfilled that promise. Those opportunities are offered to some, but not all, students. There is a predictable inverse relationship between academic outcomes and family income that even the best traditional educational delivery methods have failed to successfully address.

It doesn't matter if you are a conspiracy theorist and believe there is a plot to dismantle public education in America, or a pragmatist who wants to see better outcomes from educational organizations that spend more money per student than any other country on the planet, the conclusion is the same. Education as we know it must change.

Sustainable versions of performance-based teaching and learning have demonstrated success in changing the income/outcome paradigm. Zero dropouts is but one outcome of the practice of performance-based education. After all, you cannot teach students who don't come to school.

However, it is only one data point, and may not be the most important. Creating the best environment for each student to learn and listening carefully to personalize education for these students is by far more important.

Intent

Quite simply, the intent of a continuous and collaborative innovative practice is this: to give every student the educational environment in which they learn best and to place students based upon their academic progress, regardless of their chronological age.

It will be challenging to replicate all of these methods and culture in every district. Local conditions as well as the size, structure, and appetite for change of the district must all be taken into account. Perhaps the only alternative is to continue to try to improve existing pedagogy, methodologies, and delivery. But at what cost? At the national dropout rate average of 19 percent,[1] roughly 570,000 students in the class of 2016 will not get a high school diploma. How many of those are in your district?

But if change is no longer optional, how will you make it happen? Will you work within the system or outside of it, with it or against it? Will you lobby, or will you protest?

The practice of performance-based education can provide all of your students with the best educational environment in which to learn. If they are struggling, it gives them just-in-time remediation. When they are not, it gives them accelerated learning.

This proficiency-based methodology and culture gives your children a chance to try a wide range of career options and gives them the chance to learn and practice the skills that will make them successful in life regardless of their future choices. Can you promise the same from your existing practice?

Leaders

District leaders need to believe in the promise of performance-based education and be committed to it. There are some quick wins that can be scored (like a zero-dropouts policy) and others that must be works in progress (like accelerated education).

Communication

While the commitment is absolute, the messaging surrounding the transition should be a dialogue, not a monologue. Communication must flow easily in both directions. For example, it is amazing how many districts restrict communications to leadership by not publishing telephone numbers or e-mail addresses for the district. The role of communication is to model transparency and authenticity in order to build trust within the community. Where is the trust and transparency if district executives have to be protected from the public they serve?

Support

Staff support is crucial for the conversion to performance-based learning. It is the staff that will do the heavy lifting. They will need to be convinced and inspired that this is good for their students. Once convinced that this will make a difference in the outcomes of their students, most will be willing to try.

Community support is also paramount to accomplishing a change of this magnitude. A board that is less than enthusiastic, a media outlet that is critical, a portion of the school community that feels unsupported can each lead to a less than optimal situation. One of the resources for creating a supportive community is the *Citizen Participation Handbook.*[2]

Scope

While the changes can be phased in, it must be clear from the beginning that they are intended to be district-wide and not isolated and ultimately unsupported pockets of innovation. Large districts don't have to change to performance-based learning all at once, but there should be an expressed intent to expand to the entire district within three to four years.

One version of performance-based, student-centered learning has been described to you. There are a variety of other programs being tried throughout the country. One version is a project-based group of schools called EdVisions that is headquartered in Henderson, Minnesota. Some districts may choose to implement only a part of the program described. The results will still be positive, although perhaps not as dramatic as those that choose to implement the entire program.

Strategy and Reach

If performance-based learning is better for students and you can explain how it is better, then it will make sense for most students and parents. This is the primary strategic element. If the changes don't pass that litmus test, they will be subject to internal and external criticism and ultimately fail.

The reach should be deep into the classrooms. If the results are not optimum and you still have students that give up, then it is classroom practice that must change. Performance-based learning changes the way content is delivered. It changes classroom practice.

Timing

Begin immediately. Adopt a zero-dropouts policy and begin discussing how pedagogy might change to personalize the educational environment and place each student where they can learn best. Continue implementing performance-based learning until you leave or retire. There are means and methods described in the book that will take several school years to refine and others that can be implemented right away.

Continuum

Engage and include all district staff in this effort. Develop an expectation that the methodologies put in place are long term. Performance-based, student-centered learning is not only an eye-opening experience but also one that modifies career plans. Many teachers will say that it is so rewarding that if they could not continue teaching in this way, they would have to leave the profession.

Staffing

That said, some of the existing staff will no doubt choose to leave for various reasons. Some who are eligible for retirement may decide that they are unwilling to change. Others may see the work as too difficult and seek employment elsewhere.

However, many will be energized by the new vision and the opportunities to collaborate. Be clear when "on-boarding" new hires that this is not education as usual. And conduct a second workshop after they have been there about a month. New staff may not realize that others are facing the same issues. A second work session will reinforce that they are not alone and may help identify areas in which additional support is needed. Consider pairing veteran and novice teachers for intervals for support as well.

Assessment and Analysis

Continuous assessment and analysis is necessary for performance-based learning to be implemented. These are continuous formative assessments, with summative assessments in intervals. Teachers must know which techniques are working and which are not. Students must be aware of their current progress and be involved in determining their future. In the absence of real information, most students are optimistic about their progress and how much they have learned. How many of your students are usually surprised at their grades?

Logistics

Identifying all of the processes, steps, and dependencies will require a skillful project manager. If there is not one on staff, hire someone with this expertise to manage the work. You should have at least two pieces of information—a process map for each major initiative and a Gantt chart to place activities and events on a time schedule. The project manager must be given sufficient influence to get others in the district to willingly comply.

Mistakes

Thinking that performance-based education is just too hard to scale up, too expensive, too time-consuming, or too radical. The mistake is not giving your children the opportunity to fully experience the joy of learning.

Some Points to Remember for Future Implementation

- Education should provide opportunities, not barriers. Education should be personalized and student centered.
- The income/outcome paradigm must be addressed.
- Zero dropouts is but one outcome of a successful performance-based education system.
- Staff and community support is needed for success.
- Avoid long-term pilot projects. The conversion to project-based education should be district-wide.
- Even though the transition can be phased, a time frame for completion should be established and made public.
- There will be some turnover among staff. Make sure that new staff members understand what is planned and are well prepared for it.
- Knowledge of progress gives students control of their academic journey. Continuous assessment provides that data.
- Hire an effective project manager for this conversion, and give them executive authority.

NOTES

1. "School Districts." The United States Census Bureau. June 15, 2012. https://www.census.gov/did/www/schooldistricts/ (accessed August 30, 2015).
2. Bleiker, Hans, Annamarie Bleiker, and Jennifer Bleiker. *Citizen Participation Handbook*. Monterey: Institute for Participatory Management and Planning, 2012.

About the Author

Michael K. Raible has worked in education for more than two decades, serving as a member of the executive staff for two school districts and as CEO of his own firm, The School Solutions Group. In his practice, Raible connects verbal, visual, and audio imagery to help clients be specific about their goals and improve key processes to reach those goals. He lives with his family in Charlotte, North Carolina.